Chris Richardson

Wicked Problems
Essays for Aspiring Catholic School Leaders

Don Bosco Publications

Don Bosco Publications
Thornleigh House, Sharples Park, Bolton BL1 6PQ
United Kingdom

ISBN 978-1-909080-63-8
©Don Bosco Publications 2020
©Chris Richardson

The moral rights of the author have been asserted.

All rights reserved. No part of this publication may be reproduced, stored in a retrieval system or transmitted in any form or by any means without the prior permission in writing of Don Bosco Publications. Enquiries concerning reproduction and requests for permissions should be sent to The Manager, Don Bosco Publications, at the address above.

Front cover illustration by @sai_abhinivesh/unsplash.com

Printed in Great Britain by Jump DP

Contents

Introduction 1
Chapter One: The Church and Wicked Problems 5
Chapter Two: Catholic Schools and A Catholic Way of Seeing the World ...13
Chapter Three: Catholic Leadership in Catholic Schools 21
Chapter Four: Pastoral Care in Catholic Schools 29
Chapter Five: What Makes Our Schools Catholic? 37
Chapter Six: Priests and People: Bound by Mutual Need 45
Chapter Seven: Lay Ministry: A Developing and Growing Reality ..53
Chapter Eight: Teaching as Ministry 63
Chapter Nine: A Catholic Curriculum 71
Chapter Ten: Spiritual Development in Catholic Schools 79
Chapter Eleven: Dialogue: More Than a Friendly Chat 89
Chapter Twelve: Eucharist: Sacrificial Memorial and Sacred Banquet 97
Chapter Thirteen: Evangelisation: Looking for Mission-Effectiveness 105
Chapter Fourteen: Moral Theology: What Happened to Sin? 113
Chapter Fifteen: The Catholic School Landscape 126
Chapter Sixteen: Leadership of Service: Letting Go 131
Chapter Seventeen: Ordinary Catholic Theology 139

Introduction

These essays were originally published in 'The Pastoral Review' over a period of four years. Some were reflections on topics that I taught as part of the MA in Catholic School Leadership at St Mary's University, Twickenham. Others were modifications of larger, more specifically academic studies often stimulated by current debates within the Church.

The essays are either directly concerned with policy and practice in Catholic schools or discuss other theological issues that Catholic teachers may want to reflect upon.

The opening chapter, from which the book's title is taken, looks at 'wicked problems'. Although it was not written with schools in mind, it is a concept that has relevance to Catholic schools and highlights some of the conflicting opinions that exist on key issues in the life of the Catholic Church.

I have spent nearly all my life in Catholic institutions. I went to a Catholic primary school when I was four years old and then on to a Catholic boys' grammar school. I did my teacher training at a Catholic college and spent thirty-eight years teaching in Catholic secondary schools, the last twelve as headteacher of an 11–18 mixed Catholic comprehensive school. I was then appointed Director of Schools for the Catholic Diocese of Portsmouth, and after I retired continued to contribute to the MA in Catholic School Leadership as an associate lecturer at St Mary's Catholic University in Twickenham.

My career spans a period of significant change for the Catholic Church and for its schools. I grew up and spent my school years in a Tridentine Church. I served in my local church, learnt all the Latin responses and enjoyed the pomp and theatre of the liturgy. There were sixteen secular clergy teaching at my secondary school when I first arrived: men in Roman collars and cassocks. As far as I was aware, all the boys at the school were Catholics, and I did not know anyone who did not go to Mass on Sunday.

Vatican II was taking place during my final school years, and by the time I started teaching a number of changes had already taken place, most noticeably to the liturgy. What followed was an extended period of debate about the direction that the Church should take and the language that it should use to convey its message. There was a move away from the abstract propositional language so familiar before the Council. This was replaced by a more secular language which reflected the experience of the faithful.

This inevitably caused conflict between those who disliked the changes and those who embraced them. In these essays, I have tried to cross the divide between these two camps. They do not represent an either/or but a both/and. They both play their part in the Catholic tradition.

In using contemporary language, it is always important to ensure that the reader understands what you are trying to convey. There is a danger in trying to attribute a new meaning to familiar words. People often don't understand the change and are then misled. Like many teachers, I tried to develop a new language and probably failed. These essays are the fruit of much trial and error.

A wise bishop once told me that he was suspicious of people who used too much theological language. He wondered whether they knew what they were talking about. Taking this caution to heart, I have avoided technical theological language where possible and explained what I mean by it when it is used. I hope that people will find this helpful and not feel patronised by it.

Catholic schools have changed greatly during my career. When I started teaching, the Local Authority managed the budget and the classroom was a secret garden. Then came Local Management of Schools, where the headteacher had to manage the budget. The Great Education Reform Act of 1988, which introduced a National Curriculum was followed shortly afterwards by the introduction of inspections by the newly created Office for Standards in Education, Ofsted.

Now schools were operating in a marketplace where money followed pupils, results were published and became the measure of success. This was a challenge for Catholic schools because it endangered the holistic Catholic educational mission including its preferential outreach to the poor and marginalised. These essays reflect the tensions inherent in trying to balance success in secular terms and faithfulness to the Church's educational mission.

With the exception of the opening chapter, I have arranged the essays in the order in which they were published rather than rearranging them into a more logical pattern. This is because my thinking developed over time, and it seems more honest to present them this way. Consequently, the Catholic schools landscape comes last when it should, more logically, come first.

There are some recurring themes. I decided not to make changes in order to remove them as they probably represent core concepts as far as I am concerned and benefit from repetition. An example is the mantra that 'the person the child is becoming is more important that what he or she knows'. I picked this up at a conference in the 1970s and it has stayed with me through my career, appearing in any prospectus that I wrote as a headteacher. I think that it captures an important aspect of the Catholic educational endeavour. It occurs more than once in these essays.

I would like to record my thanks to 'The Pastoral Review' for publishing my essays. When I began writing them the editor was Rev Professor Michael Hayes, who had been my PhD supervisor, and I was grateful for his encouragement. Sadly, Michael was called to the Lord in 2017. His successor as editor, Dr Anthony Towey, has been kind enough to continue to accept my offerings.

CHAPTER ONE

The Church and Wicked Problems

Not a Crisis

The word 'crisis' has been heard in Church circles more and more over the last decade. Encouragingly, it was missing from reports on the Extraordinary Synod of Bishops on the Family. The publication of the *relatio* halfway through the Synod caused the usual flurry of excitement and expectation among the media and those anxious to see a more pastoral approach to the divorced and a more inclusive approach to homosexuals. There was also dismay and even anger among those who saw the proposals as incompatible with scripture and tradition and a betrayal of those who adhered faithfully to Church teaching.

Unusually the result was not a complete anticlimax. The whole process adopted by the Synod and its continuation through a further period of reflection and debate before it resumes this October can be seen as a recognition that the Church is not dealing with crisis but with something else. Something that planners call a 'wicked problem'.

Dealing with Problems

Everyday problems, like ensuring Mass will be available at the parish church during the parish priest's vacation or how to manage now that the sacristan has retired, pose no serious difficulty. They are what planners call 'tame' problems because there is at least one obvious solution and it just has to be implemented. Unlike these tame problems, a crisis, where something valued is in imminent danger of being lost, requires a different response. Planners call these 'critical' problems and they require strong leadership along with positive action to tackle the problem. Solutions are found that address causes which have been identified and are assumed to be correct. These solutions are often promoted as self-evident. Disparate voices and opinions are not appreciated, and everyone is called upon to rally in support of the leader and the chosen strategy.

Wicked Problems

Planners and social scientists are familiar with another class of problem, where not only the causes are uncertain, but the solutions are also illusive. These are the 'wicked problems'. The description 'wicked' arises from their intractability and does not represent an ethical judgement. Wicked problems are complex, and it is difficult to disentangle causes and effects. The problem has no single definition but is subject to multiple subjective interpretations. There is no clear solution to the problem, and many possible and partial solutions compete with each other for recognition. To make matters worse, it is not really possible to see what a solution would look like or to know whether you have solved the problem. Put succinctly, a wicked problem "has innumerable causes, is tough to describe, and doesn't have a right answer."[1]

The Church Crisis as a Wicked Problem

The situation that the Church finds itself in seems to correspond closely with a wicked problem. In nearly every gathering of Catholics, where discussions turn to problems faced by the Church, people will offer their favoured cause with a straightforward solution. Some people will say that young people don't come to church because they are bored, and the solution is livelier, more relevant liturgies. Others will argue that the Church is unwelcoming to the divorced and remarried, and the solution is to reimagine the Church's teaching on divorce. Others will say that we offend our separated brethren by refusing to let them receive the Blessed Sacrament at Mass, and the solution is intercommunion. Simple causes with simple solutions uncomplicated by the theological reflection of the Church; what could be easier?

Contrary solutions are offered to the same problems. The decline in vocations to the priesthood can be solved by removing celibacy as a compulsory prerequisite and consequently attracting numerous married men who would otherwise be willing to serve as priests. Conversely the decline in vocations will be solved by insisting on celibacy as a countercultural sign that will attract men, who will be effective witnesses to Christ in the modern world.

Unfortunately, the Church's problems are not only more complicated that these simple solutions suggest but also more complex. The Church's problems are neither 'tame' nor 'critical' but 'wicked'. The originators of the term were two American professors of design and city planning, Horst Rittel and Melvin Webber.[2] They offered a number of features of wicked problems and it would be helpful to relate some of these to the present situation in the Church.

There is no Definitive Formulation of a Wicked Problem

It might be argued that we can state the problem quite clearly: there is a decline in active Church membership. However, defining active Church membership is not straightforward. Are we only to count those who attend Mass weekly and who also try to live out the Gospel in their lives? Are we to count those who attend Mass weekly but whose life choices are difficult to reconcile with the Church's teaching? Are we to include those who strive to live the Christian life but have little contact with the institutional Church? How are we to regard those who attend Mass regularly but not weekly? For each of these categories of people there are subcategories, for example those who are cavalier about their Mass attendance and those whose life circumstances make attendance at Mass problematic.

What are the causes of the problem? Does a decline in active Church membership indicate a decline in a belief in God? Does it represent a rejection of Jesus Christ and the principles and values taught in the Gospel? Is it caused by a lack of trust in the institutional Church and its leaders? Is it a result of the changes introduced by Vatican II or a failure to implement those changes fully? Are we still searching for a new way of expressing our beliefs that will speak to modern minds or is it the inadequacy of new expressions that have devalued the message?

How the Problem is Formulated Determines How it Will Be Solved

Immediately, it is obvious that how you understand the problem depends on what you see as the causes, many of which intersect each other and have their own causes in a complex series of interlocking circles of cause and effect. Finding possible solutions to any of these potential causes, rather than resolving the problem, often opens it up even further. Trying to meet the demands of women is a good example. To start with there is no unified voice. The spectrum of female opinion stretches from those who agree entirely with the Church that the woman has a key role to play as homemaker, through those who want a more prominent place for women in decision-making, and those who interpret the scripture from a feminine perspective, all the way to those who want to ordain women to the priesthood.

Ordaining women to the priesthood would satisfy some but, as the Church of England has already discovered, it would dismay others. There is a clear magisterial prohibition on the ordination of women. This raises questions about authority in the Church and its exercise. It raises questions about the role of obedience and the place of loyal dissent. It calls into question the tradition of the Church and how that is to be understood. Indeed, as the possible solution is explored, more problems arise. In fact, it is only by teasing out solutions that the problem is fully understood. Such are wicked problems. It is only by understanding solutions that we begin to understand the problem. How we perceive the problem will influence what we regard as possible solutions.

Every Wicked Problem is a Symptom of Another Problem

The decline in active church attendance might be seen as resulting from inadequate catechesis. Immediately we are into multiple possible causes. Let's assume that one of those causes is a loss of faith in the supernatural and a desire to express the faith in human terms. Loss of faith will itself have multiple causes, but it represents a higher-level cause than some others. In fact, it may be a significant general cause of many of the Church's problems. The higher the level of the problem then the more general will be its formulation. However, unless attempts are made to solve the higher-level problems then the lower-level problems that are essentially symptoms of the higher-level problem will not be solved.

There is No Stopping Rule

Wicked problems are not like puzzles that have a solution. You know when you have completed the puzzle. Because of the complex causal links and the relationship between defining the problem and identifying solutions, the Church's problems cannot be finally resolved. Each solution will result in further elaborations of the problem. It is hard to predict what the new problems will be until the solutions are put in place. Every solution has consequences and their repercussions move us into new areas of challenge and opportunity. Reasserting Church teaching in the face of an apparent decline in faith may be seen as a sensible thing to do. However, restricting debate and sanctioning dissenters can cause resentment and a lack of trust. Now this problem must be dealt with.

It is Difficult to Evaluate Solutions

One approach to a decline in faith is to simply accept it as the will of God and allow the Church to become smaller and hopefully, as a result, more faithful. Rather than parishes as we know then in Europe, we would have small mutually supporting communities, who have the ministry of a priest when one is available. The authentic witness of these Catholics could be the best antidote to a faithless world. An alternative view encourages a more robust and authentic evangelisation, which calls for far greater public witness to the love of God in the lives of the faithful. Which solution is best?

One might legitimately assert that it is the role of the *Magisterium*[3] to judge between possible solutions. But ultimately the role of the *Magisterium* is to secure the veracity of the deposit of faith. This does not guarantee its wisdom in deciding on solutions to particular problems. Indeed, there are those who criticise the episcopal handling of the dissemination and reception of Vatican II. There are also conflicting opinions on how the authority vested in the *Magisterium* should be exercised.

Every Solution Leaves its Mark

Wicked problems cannot be solved by a process of trial and error. Each trial changes the nature of the problem and requires a different solution. Vatican II cannot be undone without damaging the integrity of the Church. Papal pronouncements—even noninfallible ones—exert an enduring influence, being a source of reassurance for some and a barrier for others. Solutions to wicked problems have to take into account particular and distinctive circumstances. Appropriate action in Africa may be counterproductive in Europe.

Wicked problems are always unique. There may be similarities between them and previous problems but changing circumstances and people, together with the consequences of previous solutions, make relying on how we dealt with this last year inappropriate. Experience may aid judgements about which solutions to adopt, but before that stage is reached, there must be a thorough consideration of possible solutions. This requires open-ended discussions and the involvement of as many people as possible. Reserving the problem for a few trusted people to solve may keep it manageable but is unlikely to explore the breadth of possible solutions and consequently ways of understanding the problem.

Advice from Planners

All this may seem very depressing. Surely it is a recipe for paralysis brought about by over analysis. Is the suggestion that we just do nothing? In fact, what can be offered are not solutions to problems but ways of dealing with them. We can glean some advice from those who work with wicked problems.

The experience of planners is that wicked problems are not resolved—if they are ever fully resolved at all—by recourse to tried and tested methods. Experimental approaches are required and a willingness to explore ideas and see where they lead. There needs to be courage to try what is genuinely new and not just to dress up old ideas in new clothes. There is a need for a sharing of knowledge and skills right across the Church and a commitment to genuine collaboration developing a collective intelligence. This will throw up ideas that challenge existing norms, but it is necessary to embrace 'positive deviance and constructive dissent'. We must work with emerging solutions rather than suppress them. Innovation and learning from failure will require trust. Multiple partial solutions may be required. The desire to seek more data or further clarify the problem or to reduce it to smaller problems, needs to be avoided. Conventional approaches may not help, in particular, the desire to understand the problem fully first and then solve it does not apply because, as we have seen, finding solutions helps to define the problem.

The Church and Wicked Problems

A number of these suggestions are problematic for the Church. It is hard to imagine the Church embracing 'positive deviancy and constructive dissent'. However, the Fathers of Vatican II may well have pointed to some ways of dealing with wicked problems that would find favour with planners. They advocated collegiality among the bishops of the world. Whether the synods of bishops that emerged from this insight represent genuine collegiality is less certain. It may be that a fuller and richer development of collaboration might be a helpful way forward in dealing with wicked problems. The Fathers also pointed to the supernatural interpretation of the faith, the *sensus fidei*, which resided in all the people of God.[4] This was not a call for democracy or to embrace communitarianism but recognition that the experience of the faithful had a valuable part to play in the life of the Church. A richer understanding of the *sensus fidei* may help us tackle wicked problems.

The Church has another advantage when it comes to managing wicked problems. The Church is guided by the Holy Spirit. Through prayerful discernment, ways forward can emerge. But discernment, allowing the Spirit to lead us, requires open hearts and minds. The Spirit will blow as it will and lead us where it will. We have to be willing to follow even when the direction challenges the status quo.

Free and open debate may bring its risks. It is difficult to avoid an opinion which corresponds with my disposition, being regarded as correct and gathering momentum. However, it may be that within the dynamics of the debate, solutions are to be found and a fuller appreciation of the wicked problems that we face.

Endnotes

1   J. C. Camillus, 'Strategy as a Wicked Problem' in *Harvard Business Review*, May 2008. Similar problems had previously been described as Type III situations or adaptive problems. Cf. R.A. Heifetz, *Leadership Without Easy Answers*, (Cambridge, MA: The Belknap Press of Harvard University, 1994).

2   H. W. J. Rittel & M. M. Webber, 'Dilemmas in a General Theory of Planning' in *Policy Sciences* 4 (1973), 155-169.

3   This is not always an undisputed term. For long periods in the Church's history, theologians were considered to be part of the *Magisterium*. Generally, now, the term refers to the teaching authority exercised by the bishops in communion with the Bishop of Rome.

4   Cf. Pope Paul VI, Dogmatic Constitution on the Church, *Lumen Gentium* (Vatican website, 1964) [*LG*], n.12, & *Catechism of the Catholic Church* (Vatican website, 2003, original Latin version 1993) [CCC], n. 91.

CHAPTER TWO

Catholic Schools and a Catholic Way of Seeing the World

Introduction

When I visit schools, I am always struck by how different they are from each other, and not just in their physical appearance. Their aims may be very similar, but they display a variety of styles. In part these styles reflect the often-unspoken assumptions that underpin how the school operates. These same assumptions promote a distinctive attitude to life, which will permeate throughout the school, its activities and every decision that is made.[1] In other words, every school will expose their pupils to a particular way of seeing the world. There are underlying assumptions behind the education provided in every school, even those that aspire to offer an education that is free from ideological influences. Every school has a philosophy, a vision of what the school is striving to achieve. Every school has an understanding of how pupils learn and the substance and methods that it considers worthwhile and appropriate. As a result, every school passes on an understanding of the origins, nature and capacity of the human condition and how to make sense of the society, planet and universe that we inhabit.

Catholic schools are no exception. According to the Congregation for Catholic Education (CCE), they develop "a specific concept of the world, of man, and of history."[2] The Catholic way of seeing the world has distinctive features and is obliged to defend itself against other competing philosophies of life. Indeed, as the late Cardinal Hume argued forcefully, we are "fighting for the minds and imaginations of the young, offering rival views of human fulfilment and happiness."[3]

Clarity in A Place of Dialogue

Children live in a world where they experience a plurality of life choices. They come across people with attitudes and assumptions that are not the same as their own. However, many children have very little idea of what a Catholic worldview might be. Catholic schools endeavour to expose them to what a Catholic way of life has to offer and the implications of belief in a creator God for our understanding of ourselves and other people. Catholic schools are inevitably places where a secular worldview and a religious worldview enter into dialogue with each other. Uniquely among such places of dialogue in society, the Catholic school provides an environment where the Catholic position can expect to be given a respectful hearing.[4] The success of such a dialogue will differ from school to school and depend on a complex of factors including the level of Catholic practice of constituent families, the witness of Catholic staff, the availability of clergy and lay chaplains and the leadership of the headteacher. Bearing witness is of great importance. and often it is this witness to the faith that sustains our schools. Effective witness tells its own story. However, there is also a need to articulate that story by making explicit what it means to be a Catholic and what is distinctive about the way that Catholics see the world.

The 'What' As Well As The 'How'

What then does the Catholic school say of itself? How does it articulate its presuppositions? My own contact with headteachers over many years leaves me in no doubt about their faith in God and God's providence. They live life in the presence of a real but almost taken for granted God. They talk about the centrality of Jesus Christ in their own lives and that of their school. Christ is the model that they are proposing to their students and trying, however inadequately, to model in their lives. Relationships are crucial in their understanding of their faith, and developing relationships based on explicit Gospel values is a theme that returns regularly in their narratives about their work. Although they do not refer to it as such, they have a clear incarnational understanding that underpins their recognition that Christ is present in and through all members of the school community. They are generally loyal to the institutional Church, despite its perceived weaknesses. Their central focus on Jesus Christ, relationships, encountering God in created things, Christ present among us and commitment to the Church underpin their educational endeavours and the vision of reality that they are offering to their pupils.[5] These perspectives are central to the Catholic tradition but are generally expressed in what one might call anthropological language, as it arises from our understanding of the human condition. Their emphasis is on 'how' to be a Christian not on 'what' it means to be a Christian.[6]

Providing A Coherent Account

Catholic education is traditionally holistic or, as the CCE puts it, is concerned with "integral formation."[7] This integral formation is not concerned primarily with empirically verifiable outcomes but is designed to allow its recipients to contribute to the society in which they live, to promote the common good and to seek the Kingdom both in this life and the next.[8] Catholic schools are concerned with developing people as people[9] and not with turning them into units of production in the workplace. The challenge for Catholic schools is to maintain the integrity of their mission[10] within a system that seems to privilege certain aspects of learning and a narrow way of measuring success. Schools have to avoid the temptation to emphasise those elements of what they offer that are valued more generally in society whilst relegating distinctively Catholic features to the margins, or simply becoming a state school conducted in premises provided by the Catholic Church.[11]

Catholic schools must provide a coherent and explicit account of a Catholic way of seeing the world that informs their educational mission. What is a Catholic way of seeing the world? What are the underlying assumptions that inform the life of our schools? There are, no doubt, many ways of expressing these.[12] What is offered here is a grouping of main themes that the author has found helpful.

Catholic Life is a Purposeful Life

Life is purposeful, and education is not just an aimless meander through an unknown landscape—"full of sound and fury, signifying nothing"[13]—

but has a particular destination in mind. Life's goal is union with God. The Christian anthropology that drives this sense of purpose recognises that we are created by God, redeemed by Christ and destined for eternal life. We are not authors of our own history as contemporary society seems to believe. We are dependant creatures, who grow to fulfilment by the grace (or love) of God. Understanding this colours our approach to education in many ways, not least in our recognition that ends are more important than means, and that if means are confused with ends, the resulting education is deficient. Yes, gaining skills and qualifications is important but those attributes are only a means to further ends. The person the child is becoming is more important than what he or she knows. This makes education a moral endeavour because it is not just concerned with helping people acquire skills and knowledge but also with providing a moral compass with which to analyse and use them.

Catholic Life is a Life of Faith: A Life Where We Embrace Mystery

There are things that we know by faith that cannot be reconciled with secular knowledge. Or, at least, the scientific method and the language of contemporary thought are inadequate for speaking of these things. We can and do try to give expression to them using language that has currency in the modern world, but there is always a danger that the language that we use will retain its original meaning for our hearers, giving them the impression that we are only making secular claims. Catholic schools must help pupils learn 'what' it means to be a Catholic as well as 'how' to live the Christian life. Pupils need knowledge as well as experience. To understand the life of faith one must enter into it. Catholic schools offer their students an opportunity to experience this life of faith but must take care that what is offered is not a sanitised experience, devoid of mystery. There is no compulsion on students to accept the life of faith, but their choices will be coloured by experience. Crucial to their experience of the life of faith will be the witness of their teachers, who walk with them and share their faith and faithfulness.

Catholic Life is Underpinned by a Sacramental Imagination

Catholics believe that everything that God created is good. We see the influence of the creator present in the world. We encounter the creator in created things. They become signs or sacraments of a God, who transcends them and who we can't see.[14] In particular, we recognise that the people in our schools are all made in the image of God and are unique and of infinite value. Catholic schools are concerned with helping each person, child and adult, recognise his or her own worth and the worth of others. This has implications for how our schools are led and managed. Catholics accept that Jesus Christ is the greatest sign of the encounter between the divine and the human. As a consequence, Jesus must be at the heart of a Catholic school. He is the "way the truth and the life" (Jn 14:6), and by coming to know him better, we come to know more about ourselves.

Catholic Life is Communal

Catholic schools are not simply communities of individuals who cooperate for mutual advantage or emotional support. It is in their understanding of community as a relationship between people and God that their greatest strength is to be found. Catholics know that community is necessary for human flourishing. Taking the Trinity as a model of reconciled difference,[15] Catholic communities are catholic, embracing everyone and especially the troubled and troublesome. There is recognition that relationships are important. If we are to have an authentic relationship with the Lord, then we must learn to develop relationships with other members of the community. These relationships should be characterised by mutual respect and cooperation. Catholic schools are also communities, where members are encouraged to make Christ present for each other. Not only does our understanding of the importance of community influence the way that we see the world, but it also provides us with a significant resource, with the schools generally enjoying support from within and without the extended Catholic community of the school.

Catholic Life is Ecclesial

Catholic schools are effectively agencies of the Catholic Church. They contribute to the Church's work of salvation. It is in and through the Church that Catholics can live the life of faith most fully. Here they can experience community as communion. Here they can share their experience of the living Lord with others and in the light of the Church's understanding accumulated over the years. Here the grace of God is made most powerfully available to them. Catholic schools offer an experience of Church and must be authentic witnesses to what the Church is and what is has to offer. Catholic schools must remain faithful to the *Magisterium* of the Church under whose auspices they function.

Catholic Life is Missionary

At the end of Mass each Sunday we are sent out to bear witness to Christ in the world. Catholic schools model this in the way that they cooperate with other local schools in pursuit of the common good. Here, in the public arena where teachers meet together or schools compete with each other, they have an opportunity to bring something distinctive to the educational enterprise. The missionary life is also a life of service. Excellence is pursued so that its fruits can be shared. Solidarity with the poor and disadvantaged is expressed in action not just words. Confidence is balanced with humility and a willingness to share what we value with others, whilst benefitting from what they can share with us.

Conclusion

These insights into the Catholic life and how they influence Catholic schools are personal and no doubt reflect my own theological disposition. Other people would legitimately stress other aspects of the Catholic life. The reflection involved in arriving at these is what is important. If Catholic schools are to promote a distinctive attitude to life, it is important that those who lead them can clearly articulate what that distinctive attitude is. If it can only speak of itself in terms of values that any local school would also claim to promote and is unable to express a distinctively Catholic understanding of the human condition that underpins its work and influences how it operates, then its capacity to offer a rival concept of human existence, fulfilment and happiness will be diminished.

Endnotes

1   Congregation for Catholic Education (CCE), *The Catholic School*, (London: CTS, 1977), n. 29.

2   ibid., n. 8.

3   B. Hume, 'The Church's Mission in Education' in *Partners in Mission: A Collection of Talks by Bishops on Issues Affecting Catholic Education*, (London: CES, 1997), p. 24.

4   L. Boeve, 'The Identity of a Catholic University in Post-Christian European Societies: Four Models', *Louvain Studies* 31, (2006), pp. 238-258.

5   Cf. C.J. Richardson, *The Theological Disposition of Lay Catholic Headteachers: Evidence from Two English Dioceses*. (Saarbrücken: LAP LAMBERT Academic, 2012).

6   C.J. Richardson, *The Theological Disposition of lay Catholic Headteachers*, Unpublished PhD Thesis, (St Mary's University College, Twickenham, 2011).

7   CCE, *The Catholic School*, n. 26.

8   God's Kingdom is where His will is done. If we seek the Kingdom, then we accept God's jurisdiction over our lives and try to build a society based on justice and peace here on earth whilst anticipating its fulness when Christ comes again.

9   See J.C. Conroy, '"The Long Johns" and Catholic Education' in J.C. Conroy (ed), *Catholic Education Inside-Out and Outside-In*, (Dublin: Veritas, 1999), p. 47.

10   G. Grace, *Catholic Schools: Mission, Markets and Morality*, (London: Routledge Falmer, 2002), pp. 178, 235 & 237.

11   K. Treston, 'Ethos and identity: Foundational concerns for Catholic schools' in R. Keane & D. Riley (eds), *Quality Catholic Schools*, (Brisbane: Brisbane Catholic Education, 1997), p. 17.

12   For the distinctively Catholic see R. McBrien, *Catholicism*, (New York: HaperCollins, 1994), pp. 8-16. For a Catholic way of seeing the world see T. H. Groome, 'What Makes A Catholic School,' in T. McLaughlin, et al. (eds), *The Contemporary Catholic School: Context, Identity and Diversity*, (London: Falmer Press, 1996), pp. 117/118. For essentials of Catholic education see D. Konstant, et al. *Signposts and Homecomings*, (London: St Paul, 1981), pp. 119-121. For underlying assumptions behind Catholic schooling see R.M. Jacobs, *The Grammar of Catholic Schooling* (Washington DC: National Catholic Educational Association, 1997).

13   W. Shakespeare, *Macbeth*, Act 5, scene 5, lines 26-27.

14   For a further reflection on the sacramental imagination see the section on 'Sacramental Nature of Ministry' in Chapter Eight 'Teaching as Ministry'.

15   Cf. J. Millbank, *Theology and Social Theory: Beyond Secular Reason*, (London, Blackwell, 1990), pp. 434-438.

CHAPTER THREE

Catholic Leadership in Catholic Schools

Introduction

The use of observation and measurement as a means of improving productivity was first introduced by Frederick Winslow Taylor[1] at the beginning of the 20th century, an approach known as scientific management. Since then the sheer volume of material being produced on leadership and management has grown exponentially. Fortunately, much of the advice given in these books is similar, and a reasonably coherent pattern of development in leadership theory can be identified. Initially the emphasis was on efficient organisation, with workers no more than cogs in a wheel. Leadership was essentially about command and control. Over time, researchers discovered that people became more committed to their work and more productive if they felt that their contribution was valued and that their opinions were taken into account. It became evident that leadership was essentially about relationships.

Here, then, is the meeting place between Catholicism and leadership. Both are essentially about relationships. However, whereas leadership theory recognises a range of approaches to leadership that can be learnt, the underlying features of Catholic leadership are dispositional. The Catholic leader will no doubt make good use of ways of leading and managing that have proven successful elsewhere and are underpinned by reliable research, but they will always modify them in the light of enduring attitudes of mind that have been nurtured within a Catholic environment.

My own experience is in Catholic schools and so I feel more confident in writing about leadership in this context. However, if my contention that key features of Catholic leadership are dispositional is correct, then what applies in schools will apply elsewhere.

Schools in general are seen as requiring leadership at all levels. In the most successful schools, all members of staff have leadership roles and their views are valued and influence how the school operates. The more extensive the level of mutual commitment and accountability, the better the quality of leadership and management is judged to be. There is considerable evidence both from research and anecdote that effective collaboration, which benefits from a wide variety of effectively coordinated skills and experience, enriches the overall quality of provision.

Making sure that this type of leadership is developed and effective is the responsibility of the headteacher. Despite the development of distributive leadership models in schools and greater collaboration among staff, there is little doubt that the headteacher plays a crucial role in the ethos and success of a school.[2] The headteacher's influence, for good or ill, permeates a school. In a Catholic school the commitment of the headteacher to the religious dimension of the school will determine the importance given to this by others in the school. What is true of the headteacher is also true, to a lesser extent, of others who exercise leadership within the school.

In schools, as is probably the case in most professions, adherence to, and even enthusiasm for, prevailing methods is an essential prerequisite for professional advancement. The ever-present spectre of Ofsted encourages headteachers to adopt nationally recognised approaches to leadership in pursuit of standards of delivery and attainment that do not always pay much regard to the social and psychological needs of the pupils in the school. The challenge for Catholic leadership is to ensure that the school is seen to be effective when measured against national standards whilst remaining authentically Catholic. Catholic leadership balances 'being successful' with 'being faithful'.

Pastors of Souls

A leader in a Catholic school has a responsibility as a pastor of souls. The example that they give must help others to understand what it means to be a Catholic. The Church recognises the importance of the teacher as someone who lives out their Christian vocation in the midst of everyday life.[3] As such, a teacher provides a role model of how to be a Christian in the world with all the challenges and uncertainties, along with the joys and opportunities that this involves. Leaders provide a similar example to their colleagues. By the way that they lead, they help others understand what it means to be a Catholic and draw them closer to Christ.[4] It is an awesome responsibility. Just as Jesus warns his disciples against leading people astray (Matt 5:19), so, too, must the leader in a Catholic school avoid this danger. This is not easy. Difficult decisions have to be made. Disciplinary action has to be taken from time to time, even with members of staff. Jesus challenges the wrongdoer but always offers reconciliation and a new beginning. He forgives the adulterous woman and tells her to sin no more (Jn 8:1–11).

How are Catholic leaders to balance the ability of a teacher to achieve classroom targets against the contribution that this teacher makes in another aspect of the life of the school, perhaps as someone who young people can confide in or who makes Christ present for others? Such dilemmas are exacerbated by a system obsessed with delivering programmes designed to achieve pupil attainment targets rather than helping them become fully rounded, emotionally intelligent, ethically grounded, mature Christian people. It is, of course, a mistake to see academic achievement and holistic development as opposites. However, ensuring that the one does not overshadow the other is not always easy.

The leader must be a sign of Christ's presence in the community, an "Icon of Christ."[5] They must speak out against those things that cannot be reconciled with the Gospel and review their own decision-making and behaviour against this standard. They must also promote the building up of God's Kingdom. In these ways, David O'Malley[6] sees them as fulfilling their baptismal vocation as priest, prophet and king.

Leadership as Service

In the Gospel Jesus makes it clear that service is the distinguishing feature of Christian leadership (Lk 21:24–27). The master washes his disciples' feet and they are cautioned against lording it over their followers as secular rulers do (Lk 22:26). It is not unusual for Christians to speak of Jesus as the 'Servant King'. But this is not the service of someone who is forced to do the will of another. It is not being at someone else's beck and call or providing whatever another wants. It is having a real and enduring concern for the good of the other. It is a desire to see people realise the fullness of life that Jesus came to give them. From the various qualities which characterise servant leadership,[7] the two that are particularly relevant to the Catholic leader are humility and sacrifice. Servant leaders are not concerned for their own aggrandisement nor do they take the credit for all that is achieved. They shine a light on the success of others.

Servant leadership is not a 'style' that can be learnt or a management tool that can be used or discarded as necessary. Servant leadership is dispositional. It is the leaders' default position; their natural instinct is to serve. They genuinely value others and seek their well-being and growth as the people that God intended them to be. A servant leader can be assertive and can take charge. They can make difficult decisions that don't always find favour with others. However, decision-making is underpinned by discernment based on prayerful reflection, justice is always tempered with mercy, and criticism offered without rancour and as a precursor to constructive advice.

Love

Jesus commands us to respond to his love for us by loving one another (Jn 15:12). The early Christian communities were known for exhibiting this love. Love is demanding, it is patient and kind, is not easily angered, keeps no records of wrongs, always protects, trusts, hopes, and perseveres. Love never fails (cf. 1 Cor 13: 4–7). The Catholic leader cannot put aside love to suit the circumstances. Love is a necessary component of service. The service given is not that of the resentful slave but of the lover. Greenleaf, who introduced the term 'servant leadership' into the lectionary of leadership theory, argued that love required an unlimited liability for another person. As soon as that liability was qualified, love was diminished.[8]

Christian love, often referred to by its Greek name *agape*, is an unselfish love. It is also *caritas*, which Pope Benedict XVI taught is love that is received from God and given to others.[9] Love is "a giving experience, a selfless act,"[10]

This is not easy. Some people are difficult to like, let alone love. But it is to the least loveable that the Catholic leader has a special responsibility. Here the preferential option for the poor and marginalised finds tangible expression in the life and work of the Catholic leader. Some people are difficult to lead and can be seen as burdensome. Love enables the leader to carry this burden and hopefully to gradually find it lighter as a greater degree of mutual trust and respect develop. Max Dupree puts this succinctly, and with echoes of the Christian calling to carry our cross, when he writes that "leaders don't inflict pain, they bear it."[11]

Love does not excuse the leader from the need for tough and even unpopular decisions. Pursuing competency or disciplinary procedures may not appear to be the act of a lover. Telling someone that they are not really called to be a teacher may be an act of loving service that will preserve their dignity and allow them to find an alternative occupation which they will find more fulfilling, but it is nevertheless painful advice to give or receive. It is not about being cruel to be kind. It is never kind to be cruel. However, love provides a moral compass which guides decision-making and regulates relationships between people. The difficult balancing act requires concern for the person to accompany a professional critique of their work. As Benedict XVI reminded us, with reference to St Paul (Eph 4:15), charity and truth are inseparable.[12]

The Dignity of The Individual

Each member of the school community shares in the life of God and is unique and of infinite value. Leaders must respect the dignity of the individual (including staff, parents and Ofsted Inspectors) as a child of God. As Pope St John Paul II taught in his encyclical on work, "it is the dignity that belongs to people that gives dignity and value to everything that they do."[13] The work that people do must "fulfil the calling to be a person."[14] As James Hanvey points out, a school must "...give space to humanity, nourishing it as well as trying to harness and direct it."[15]

The implications of this are significant. Not only does it influence the way that people are treated at an interpersonal level but also the quality of the work that they are asked to do. If members of staff are routinely required to wait beyond scheduled appointments with the headteacher, what message are they being given about their relative value? How can one justify inhibiting professional ambitions, knowingly or unthinkingly, by denying appropriate training or opportunities to develop new skills and gain new experiences? How can one justify allowing a colleague to carry too heavy a workload because finding an alternative solution would be unaffordable?

A Gifted People

Each member of the school community has received particular gifts from God and has a part to play in the divine plan. Leaders must help them identify these gifts and encourage them to develop and share them. St Paul identifies the different roles that people play in the Christian community. He develops the concept of Church as the Body of Christ. Each part of the body, however humble or apparently insignificant, is vital for the wellbeing of the whole (1 Cor 12:12-30). For the leader, the challenge is to value a wide variety of contributions that vary in quality. Catholic leaders are not dismissive of certain opinions because they do not fit in with the prevailing orthodoxy. The apparently irrelevant may offer some new insight. The minor players receive thanks and affirmation, not only the major players. The voice of the Spirit can be heard in the contribution of the least experienced or assertive.[16]

Idealistic Rubbish

Is this simply idealistic rubbish? Do leaders in Catholic schools live up to these aspirations and display these characteristics on a daily basis? I think that many of them do. Do they always get it right? Almost certainly not. We all fail to live up to the fullness of our Christian vocation in so many ways. Such is the weakness of the human condition. But unless we reflect on the kind of leadership that we are striving to provide, it is very easy for us to be subverted by pragmatics and find that we are no longer truly Catholic leaders at all.

The Catholic leader, in school or in any other Catholic setting, may be tempted to focus their attention on the good of the students or of the institution overall.

This is no doubt both laudable and justifiable. However, this primary focus should not be used as mitigation for leadership of individuals that fails to live up to what is expected of a Catholic leader. Nor are these expectations the exclusive burden of headteachers. They apply to everyone who exercises leadership, at whatever level, in Catholic school, parishes, association or religious communities. They apply to laity, religious and clergy. The higher the calling, the greater the requirement to model authentic Catholic leadership. We must never fail to pray for our leaders. A great deal is expected of them.

Endnotes

1   F.W.Taylor, *Scientific Management*, (New York: Routledge, 2003). This includes 'Shop Management' (1903), 'The Principles of Scientific Management' (1911) and 'Testimony Before the Special House Committee' (1912).

2   Cf. K. Leithwood, C. Day, P. Sammons, A. Harris, & D. Hopkins, D. *Successful School Leadership: What It Is and How It Influences Pupil Learning*, Research Report for National College of School Leadership, (Nottingham: DfES Publications, 2006).

3   Cf. CCE, *Lay Catholics in Schools: Witnesses to Faith* (Vatican website, 1982), n. 32.

4   Roisin Coll's doctoral research highlights the importance of the headteacher in the faith development of colleagues. R. Coll, 'Catholic school leadership: exploring its impact on the faith development of probationary teachers in Scotland', *International Studies in Catholic Education*, Vol. 1, No. 2, October 2009, 193–211.

5   A.M. McIntosh, *A Study of the Vision of the Catholic Primary School Head Teacher in the Light of the Leadership of Jesus Christ*, Unpublished MA Dissertation,(St Mary's University College, Twickenham, 2005).

6   D. O'Malley, *Christian Leadership in Education* (2nd Ed.), (Bolton: Don Bosco Publications, 2017), p. 24.

7   R. Greenleaf, *Servant Leadership: A journey into the nature of legitimate power and greatness*, (New York: Paulist Press, 1977). K. Punnachet, *Catholic Servant Leadership in Sisters of Saint Paul of Chartres Schools in Thailand*, PhD Thesis, (London University, Institute of Education, 2006). G Yukl, *Leadership in Organisations*, (7th Ed.), (New Jersey: Pearson, 2010).

8 R. Greenleaf, *Servant Leadership: A journey into the nature of legitimate power and greatness* (25th Anniversary Ed.), (Mahwah, NJ: Paulist, 1991), p. 2.

9 Cf. Pope Benedict XVI, *Caritas in Veritate* (Vatican website, 2009) [*CV*], n. 5.

10 B. Hume, *The Mystery of Love*, (London: Darton, Longman & Todd, 2000), p. 21.

11 M. Dupree, *Leadership is an Art*, (New York: Dell Publishing, 1989).

12 Cf. *CV*, n. 2.

13 Pope St John Paul II, *Laborem Exercens* (Vatican website, 1981), n. 22.

14 ibid., n. 20.

15 J. Hanvey, *The Spirituality of Leadership*, (London: Heythrop Institute for Religion, Ethics and Public Life, 2008), p. 13.

16 One hears echoes here from Job 32:8-9, "…it is the spirit in a mortal, the breath of the Almighty, that makes for understanding. It is not the old that are wise, nor the aged that understand what is right."

CHAPTER FOUR

Pastoral Care in Catholic Schools

Developments in Pastoral Care Over Time

When I started teaching in the early 1970s, pastoral care was beginning to become a major focus in state schools. Arguably it had always been a significant component of Catholic schooling. Through my career in Catholic education the focus of pastoral work in schools changed. Faced with large comprehensive schools where students could become anonymous, pastoral structures were put in place to create manageable cohorts and facilitate social control. Working more closely with individual students sensitised pastoral staff to individual needs. If a child's life was in turmoil, it was not surprising that they failed to participate appropriately in school. Schools began to see pastoral strategy as providing support-giving structures, which would allow the fullest development of the students.

In trying to support students educationally, socially, emotionally and vocationally, pastoral staff began to provide something akin to 'counselling' and helped students develop strategies to help themselves. With experience of trying to meet individual needs, it became clear that advice could be offered to students collectively about matters of common concern. Not only could individual needs be met in a group situation, but this work would be proactive and try to anticipate their needs. This in turn developed into a wide-ranging pastoral curriculum.

During the 1980s government was very critical of what they regarded as the lack of priority given to core subjects and the amount of time being spent on 'social work' by schools. The resulting focus on the prescribed curriculum reduced the amount of time available for a taught pastoral curriculum. It was accepted that some aspects of personal and social development deserved curriculum time and thus PSE (Personal and Social Education) was born. Over time this became a catch-all for anything that government felt schools should include in their curriculum but did not fit comfortably into traditional subjects. Gradually the number of issues that schools were expected to cover grew almost weekly. The inspection framework included issues ranging from sex education to healthy eating.

The emphasis on achievement has resulted in the change of role of heads of year in some schools where they have been replaced by 'learning mentors'. The focus of their work had been concerned with target-setting for students, tracking progress and intervention where estimated levels of attainment are not reached. Pastoral staff are engaged in helping students to develop learning strategies and to make the most of the learning opportunities that the school offers them. This work is often about motivating and raising aspiration levels.

Catholic pastoral care is always concerned with more than just the academic, important though this may be. Its orientation is determined by the long-term ambitions of a Catholic education in its fullest sense, namely, to help individuals develop into mature Christian people who can not only contribute to the society in which they live but also to fulfil their baptismal calling to fullness of life.

Catholic Pastoral Care

A definition of pastoral care that I like, probably because it resonates with my Catholic educational disposition, comes from Michael Grove in Australia. He defines pastoral care as "all measures to assist an individual person or a community reach their full potential, success and happiness in coming to a deeper understanding of their own humanity."[1]

One of the first references to pastoral care in Catholic literature is the *regulae pastoralis*, or Pastoral Rule, outlining the responsibilities of clergy or pastors, written by Pope St Gregory the Great in about 590 AD. He describes the qualities and conduct required of pastors, advocating amongst other things humility, integrity, discretion, compassion and purity of thought. Perhaps most significantly for our present purpose, Pope Gregory makes it clear that pastors must take into account individual difference when dealing with people. He also warns pastors not to ignore their own needs and to continue to nurture their own spiritual life.

Learning from The Good Shepherd

The word 'pastoral' has its roots in the Latin word *pastor*, which means shepherd (*pastoralis*, of shepherds or pastoral: *pascere*, to lead to pasture). In Christian churches the priest is often called the pastor. He is seen as the shepherd of the local flock. The prophet Ezekiel (34:12) identifies God with a shepherd who watches over his sheep. In John's Gospel (10:1–15), Jesus describes the good shepherd. The good shepherd knows the sheep by name and the sheep know the shepherd. They recognise the shepherd's voice. When difficulties arise, the shepherd does not run away as the hired help might but stays to protect the sheep. If necessary, the good shepherd will die for the sheep. The good shepherd offers the sheep "fullness of life" (Jn 10:10).

Although Jesus is not actually using this teaching to give instructions to pastors but rather to illustrate his saving mission, we can draw a number of useful insights from it. The pastoral leader will know each of their students by name. They will offer protection from harm. They may not be called to give their life for their students, but they will go the extra mile to help them. Their work involves self-sacrifice. They lead their students towards fullness of life, to become more fully human, acquiring "a deeper understanding of their own humanity",[2] and grow towards a fuller knowledge of God. All that they do must be 'life enhancing' not 'death dealing'.

Service and Love

The model of leadership offered by Jesus and one that any Christian pastoral leader should emulate is that of service (cf. Matt 20:22–28). The pastoral leader who sees their role as one of service is motivated by a desire to see their students grow and develop. Authority and even power come with the job, but the servant pastoral leader uses these for the benefit of others. The Christian pastoral leader accepts the new commandment "to love on another" (Jn 15:12) and is motivated by love. The love that one might expect to find is an unselfish and well-intentioned concern for the good of others. It is, as John Hoyle puts it, "a deep caring for other".[3] The love spoken of here is captured by the Greek word *agape*, which Pope Benedict identifies as "love grounded in and shaped by faith."[4] This is an unselfish, self-giving love. It is a central component of Catholic pastoral care.

It is important to remember that this love is not passive or sentimental. It can be challenging and demanding. In the rule of St Benedict, which was written in about 540 AD to govern life in Benedictine monasteries, the abbot is instructed to encourage the obedient, humble and patient but also to reprimand and punish the undisciplined, negligent and arrogant. St Ignatius Loyola the founder of the Jesuits spoke of discipline as 'thinking love'. So, the love that characterises pastoral care in Catholic schools is thinking love. It is the love shown by a concerned parent. It is a love that wants the best for the child. It is a love that reprimands and punishes when necessary but as St Paul tells us "it is always ready to make allowances, to trust, to hope and to endure whatever comes" (1 Cor. 13:7).

Importance of Community

Catholic teaching emphasises the importance of the community. Indeed, it recognises that relationships are essential for human flourishing. A positive life-giving community offers people a sense of belonging and makes them feel valued for who they are, not just for what they can do or achieve. Catholic schools must be about creating positive, life enhancing communities, built on trust and mutual respect.

> Good pastoral care is often associated with schools where people are respected and valued and the community dynamic, enthusiastic and vibrant. One common characteristic of such schools is the respect accorded to all persons within the community.[5]

The highly regarded research conducted by Anthony Bryk[6] and his associates in the USA found that Catholic schools outperformed other similar schools. In trying to understand why this was the case he gave one of the reasons as 'social capital'. By this he means the trusting relationships that existed within the schools and between the school and the local community and in particular the parish. Pastoral care has an important part to play in ensuring that students feel that they belong, that they are trusted and respected as individuals, and that they are seen as valuable members of the community. Pastoral care has to be concerned with building community not just supporting individuals, although the two are closely connected.

Developing the Spiritual Life

In Catholic schools there is a conscious attempt to help students develop their spiritual life. It is not possible here to unpack the full implications of this.[7] Catholic spirituality is about being animated and sustained by the knowledge that we share in the life of God, who calls us to experience the fullness of the human condition by recognising and responding to the presence of the Spirit of God in ourselves, all people and the whole of creation. Pastoral staff have an important part to play in this. Students need to be provided with opportunities for prayer and reflection and need to be encouraged to seek the presence of God in themselves and in each other. As one headteacher said to me, he looked for the face of Christ even in the naughtiest boy who was sent to his office.

Usually in Catholic schools a chaplain (often a lay person) plays a crucial part in nurturing the spiritual and religious life of the students. The role of the chaplain can vary from school to school and sometimes is shaped by the particular strengths of the incumbent. Chaplains have a pastoral role and the nature of their work often allows them to spend more time with a particular student than any other member of staff. It is important for pastoral leaders to understand the work of the chaplain and for them to work interdependently for the good of the students.

A Moral Endeavour

Two other characteristics of Catholic education seem relevant to a discussion about pastoral care. The Catholic Church has always argued that education is a moral endeavour. Without a moral compass it is impossible to judge whether the knowledge that one gains is valuable or not, whether it is life enhancing or death dealing. A student who leaves school with top grades in all subjects but who cannot tell right from wrong is unlikely to contribute to the common good. For a Catholic educator, pastoral care is concerned as much about the person the child is becoming as with what he or she knows.

Presence

Catholic education has been called a meeting of souls. Pope Pius XII, writing in about 1955, expressed his high regard for teachers and taught that they should create a close relationship between their soul and that of their student.[8] There are echoes here of the poet Kahlil Gibran who says that "the teacher who walks in the shadow of the temple among his followers, gives not of his wisdom but of his faith and his lovingness."[9] Teachers so envisaged must get to know their students, talk to them, listen to them and learn about them. They must spend time with their students and be available to them. The Salesians have a word for this. They call it 'presence' which is about 'being there' for young people—sharing time, fun, prayer, encouragement and love. It recognises the Spirit of Jesus in the hearts of the young. There are lessons here for pastoral staff.

Conclusion

There is a constantly increasing pressure on staff and students to achieve the best possible examination grades. Guidance systems that offer support for this objective are clearly an appropriate response from pastoral staff. However, there is always a danger here that the needs of the school to meet national standards will outweigh the needs of the individual, and pastoral staff must recognise and minimise this danger. Catholic pastoral care is always about nurturing the needs of the individual person and helping them not only to fulfil their academic potential but also to develop all the other gifts that God has given them. Gifts that enable them to contribute to the common good, seek the fullness of life and anticipate the eternal embrace of a loving God.

Endnotes

1   M. Grove, 'The Three R's of Pastoral care: Relationships, Respect and Responsibility' in *Pastoral Care*, June 2004, p. 34.

2   ibid.

3   J.R. Hoyle, *Leadership and the Force of Love: Six Keys to Motivating With Love*, (Thousand Oaks, California, Corwin Press, 2002), p. 3.

4   Pope Benedict XVI, *Deus Caritas Est*, (Vatican website, 2005), n. 7.

5   Grove, 'The Three R's of Pastoral care', p. 36.

6   A.S. Bryk, V.E. Lee & P.B. Holland, *Catholic Schools and the Common Good*, (Cambridge, Massachusetts & London, Harvard University Press, 1993).

7   See Chapter Ten on 'Spiritual Development in Catholic Schools'.

8   Pope Pius XII 'The Catholic Teacher, in The Benedictine Monks of Dolesmes', *Education: Papal teachings*, translated by A. Robeschini, (Boston MA, St Paul Editions, 1955), p. 534, quoted in R.M. Jacobs, *The Grammar of Catholic Schooling*, p. 53.

9   K. Gibran, *The Prophet*, (London: Heinemann, 1982), p. 67. (Originally published in 1926).

CHAPTER FIVE

What Makes Our Schools Catholic?

Striving for Excellence

On the whole, Catholic schools are successful and popular. In Surrey for example, where schools are generally very good and highly regarded, Catholic schools top the tables for academic achievement. This is highly commendable, and we should celebrate these achievements. Academic performance is important, and teachers invest huge amounts of their time and expertise helping students achieve this. Of course, it is important that young people have the skills and qualifications necessary to allow them to make a living and to live fulfilled and fulfilling lives. However, teachers are involved in something much more important. They recognise that the person the child is becoming is more important than what he or she knows.

Schools can sometimes be criticised for being one-dimensional, for concentrating too much on the cognitive, on reason and logic. There is surely little doubt that we must teach students to deduce conclusions from data, to tell fact from fiction, demonstrable truths from prejudice and opinion. I am sure our schools do all this. But there are more things in heaven and earth than facts and logic. We all have to manage our inner life. The life of imagination and feelings, the influences that inform our moral decisions and value systems, the awareness that we are not all that there is and that we are part of something greater than what we see around us. We must be open to God's invitation to break out from the confines of our own small lives and find liberation, fulfilment and salvation. What you know is only part of the person that you are becoming.

Theologically, education is seen as part of the Church's mission of salvation. Jesus came that "we may have life and have it to the full" (Jn 10:10). This is an invitation to make the most of the human condition. It is a call to be holy—to seek perfection. Consequently, we are required to strive for excellence in all that we do in our schools.

Christian Community Living

There is, however, no reference to academic performance in the Gospels and so it can be safely assumed that the main purpose of Catholic schools is not about grades. Jesus does not develop complex metaphysical concepts or abstract theological propositions—a systematic theology that would almost certainly have been beyond the grasp of most of the apostles. He tells stories, to which his audience can relate: stories of the land; stories about fig trees and vineyards; metaphors about fishing and sowing corn. He travels with them and challenges them to embrace a radical vision of what it means to do God's will. Perhaps most significantly, he gives them an experience of what we might now call Christian community living.

From this, a number of guiding principles emerge. In answer to the Pharisees, Jesus teaches that we must love God with the whole of our being—heart, soul and mind, and love our neighbour as we love ourselves (Matt 22:36–38). This, he declares, is the basis of the whole of the Law and the Prophets and is lived out by treating others as you wish to be treated (Matt 7:12). We show our love of God through prayer and worship but also by how we treat other people. By reaching out to those in need, we reach out to the Lord (Matt 25:31–46).

These three interrelated principles, loving God and neighbour, treating others as you would be treated and loving God in your neighbour, form the bedrock of a Catholic school. Here, young people are encouraged to shape their lives around love of God and neighbour. They are helped to discover how to do this in times of joy and of sorrow, when it is easy and when it is a struggle. Sometimes they succeed, sometimes they fail. A Catholic school anticipates both the success and the failure and encourages and supports the students through both experiences.

Underpinning community life is a set of values that we often call Gospel values. A helpful way of identifying these is offered by the Archdiocese of Birmingham in their document 'Christ at the Centre'.[1] Here, Fr (now Bishop) Stock derives values from the beatitudes. Among these values are included integrity, humility, compassion, justice, mercy, peace, purity of heart, service and sacrifice. We hear the words of the prophet Micah (6:8) echoing through these, "live justly, love tenderly and walk humbly with your God."

As a Christian community, the Catholic school recognises the needs of all its members, particularly those who are challenged materially, emotionally, physically, intellectually or spiritually.[2] It also takes seriously its responsibility to reach out to those in need beyond its doors[3] and work for a just and peaceful society.[4] In this way it consciously plays a small part in building the Kingdom of God.

One of the primary purposes of Catholic schools, and one that provides the foundation for the fulfilment of even more ambitious aims, is to give children an experience of Christian community living, which will influence their future lives. This Christian community is based on guiding principles, which were taught and modelled by Jesus and are underpinned by Gospel values.

Practise Virtue

These values are not just taught as an academic exercise. They are part of the fabric of the school. They underpin the work and witness of the school's leadership and the staff in general. Students not only see these values given expression by their mentors, but they are encouraged to exhibit them in their own lives. Through practise, it is hoped that these values are assimilated into the very character of the students. By practising integrity, for example, they become people of integrity. In a long tradition back through Aquinas to Aristotle, we hold that values become virtues through repetition. "Practise virtue," Pope Benedict XVI told students at the Big Assembly in the grounds of St Mary's University when he visited in 2010. He didn't just mean 'be good'. He meant develop those dispositions that are required to live life to the full.

Shared Values

Many of these values would inform good schools whether they were of a religious character or not. This is hardly surprising. The Church has had a lasting influence on Western society. Residual Christian values are still considered important although they are not always recognised as Christian and they have to contend with other value systems in the non-judgemental context of a plural society. These values would certainly be considered relevant to all Christians and could be considered as characteristic of all Christian schools.

We call our schools Catholic. Does this mean that we bring something distinctive and if so, what is it? At a time when Christians are trying to focus on what unites them rather than what separates them, it may seem inappropriate, even perverse, to identify the distinctively Catholic. However, if we claim to offer something distinctive then surely we must articulate it. Two such features seem self-evident to me.

The Living Tradition

The Church has a tradition going back 2,000 years to Christ and the apostles. Indeed, a number of its communities can trace their origins right back to the apostles. The tradition of the Church, that which is handed on from generation to generation, is not lifeless. It is not frozen at a particular point in its history. It is organic, alive. As the Church moves forward towards her ultimate goal, which is union with God, the living tradition enriches its practice and life.[5] The Catholic school embraces and embodies this tradition. It makes it real for its members, so that in the words of Pope St John XXIII the Church is "always living and always young."[6]

There sometimes appears to be a tension between the organic nature of the lived tradition and the teaching authority of the bishops. But this should be a healthy dynamic tension. Authority is an important feature of the Catholic Church and one that its schools help pupils to understand. All the faithful who have been initiated into the Church through baptism, nourished by word and sacrament and nurtured within the ecclesial community have an intuition for the faith that is a gift of the Holy Spirit. This *sensus fidei* allows them to recognise what is of the faith and what is not, as they strive to live out their

Christian lives among the "joys and hopes, griefs and anxieties"[7] of everyday life. They are guided by the teaching of the bishops, the *Magisterium*, who not only share the *sensus fidei* but also have a duty to reconcile what emerges from the lived experience of the people with the tradition of the Church.

The lived tradition involves a constant dialogue between the doctrines of the Church and the lived experience of the Christian faithful. Both these elements are important. The Church's teaching provides guidance for a journey. Experience of the journey, of living the Christian life, reinforces both the enduring relevance of the guidance and the perennial need for its clarification or even reformulation.

The people of God, lay and ordained, explore the meaning of the faith in their daily lives. Reflecting on this in prayer and, mindful of the rich tradition of the Church and the teaching of the *Magisterium*, they discern God's will, which finds expression in the teaching of the *Magisterium*. Catholic schools are places where this kind of discernment can begin to take place and the significance of both the pneumatological[8] impulse of the entire people of God and the reflective oversight of the *Magisterium* are synthesised.

A number of features of the living tradition of the Church will be evident in a Catholic school. The Church year, which forms a backdrop and rhythm to the life of the school, constantly reminds us of the life and teaching of Our Lord. As the cycle of the year unfolds, we gain a deeper understanding of the mystery of Christ. We not only remember Christ's life, death and resurrection but are invited to experience these events within the liturgy. These liturgical celebrations reflect the seasons and bind the Catholic community together in solidarity. What we celebrate is the same as what others celebrate all over the world, from north to south, from east to west; in great cathedrals and on humble makeshift altars.[9]

Signs and symbols are used to reinforce our sense of belonging and to remind us of who we are and what we profess. Most powerfully, the crucifix reminds us of our weaknesses and the lengths that Christ was prepared to go to provide us with the opportunity to overcome them. When things go wrong and we suffer in various ways, we can answer the question 'where is Jesus now' by looking at the cross and reminding ourselves that he is there suffering with us.

We pray for the living and the dead. We acknowledge a continuity between them and recognise that we are part of a complex of relationships that include the dead and the not yet born. There is breadth and depth to our beliefs.

A Eucharistic Community

Catholic schools are eucharistic communities in a number of ways. In the literal sense they are places of 'thanksgiving'. They encourage the members of their communities to recognise that all they are and all that they have are gratuitous gifts of a loving God. They acknowledge their own deficiencies and how much they rely on the love (grace) of God. In particular, they give thanks for the gift of Jesus Christ, who saved them from the corrupting weaknesses of the human condition (sin) and the finality of life as they experience it (death). They do not just see Jesus as a good role model, someone whose teaching and example they should follow, but rather as someone who challenges them to transform their lives.

Fundamental to the Catholic faith is the belief that Christ is really present on the altar in the form of bread and wine at the Eucharist during Mass. This eucharistic liturgy commemorates the death and resurrection of the Lord and is regarded as the "source and summit of the Christian life."[10] Catholic schools are eucharistic communities in the sense that they celebrate the Eucharist and invite Christ to be present among them. Members of the community have to grow in their understanding of the importance and significance of this eucharistic celebration both as a perpetuation of Christ's sacrifice on Calvary and subsequent resurrection, and as a paschal banquet, where we receive spiritual food to strengthen us in our daily lives.[11]

During the Mass, Christ is present among us through the action of the priest. By the grace of God, an ordinary man makes something extraordinary happen. In a sense, a eucharistic community is a community in which ordinary people do extraordinary things. In Catholic schools, students learn that they make Christ present to each other and consequently they should recognise the presence of Christ in each other. Heaven knows how difficult this can be. Even some parish councils struggle. But if our community life is guided by the principles and values that Jesus identified and modelled then we will get close.

Places of Dialogue

However distinctively 'Catholic' a school may be, it is unlikely that its clientele will be marked by a homogeneity of religious belief and practice. Even schools with an overwhelmingly Catholic intake are confronted with people at various stages on their faith journeys. Some come from committed practising Catholic families, who want the faith of the family reinforced and nurtured by the school. Others come from families with little active involvement in the life of faith and, despite seeking the advantages of a Catholic education, have little regard for the Church or its teachings. Other Catholic schools have a pluralist intake including Christians of other denominations, other faith traditions and those who claim to have no belief in God at all. The Church recognises the opportunity and the challenge of this fertile arena.

It is a place where dialogue can take place between people of differing beliefs, between Catholic thought and contemporary intuitions, between life as it is experienced and the Gospel as it is proclaimed. The challenge is to ensure that the Gospel is given a respectful hearing and that there are sufficient members of staff who are able to explain it authentically in word and deeds. In the best RE lessons students feel confident that they can explore their views in an atmosphere of mutual respect. Here, the Gospel perspective is clearly articulated, and students test it against other viewpoints and distinguish between well thought out positions and prejudice. In the worst RE lessons, the Gospel goes unheard due to inadequate teaching and a lack of respect for differing opinions.

Conclusion

Catholic schools are not just exam factories. They are places where young people can experience a community animated by the teaching of Jesus Christ; where the living tradition of the Catholic faith is given expression in word and deed; where Christ is made present in the liturgy and in the daily life of the school; and where young people are challenged by the Gospel and engage in dialogue with others who are exploring who and what they are called to be.

Endnotes

1   M. Stock, *Christ at the Centre: A Summary of Why the Church Provides Catholic Schools*, (Birmingham: Archdiocese of Birmingham Schools Commission, 2005).

2   CCE, *The Catholic School on the Threshold of the Third Millennium*, (Vatican website, 1997), nn. 1, 6 & 15.

3   Cf. CCE, *Educating Today and Tomorrow: A Renewing Passion, Instrumentum Laboris*, (Vatican Website 2014), n. III a.

4   Cf. Pope Paul VI, *Gaudium et Spes* (Vatican website, 1965) [*GS*], n. 39.

5   Pope Paul VI, *Dei Verbum* (Vatican website, 1965) [*DV*], n. 8.

6   Pope St John XXIII, *Humanae Salutis*, (Vatican Website, 1961), n. 7.

7   *GS*, n.1.

8   Concerning the Holy Spirit.

9   Cf. Pope St John Paul II, *Ecclesia De Eucharistia*, (Vatican website, 2003) [*EE*], n.8.

10   *LG*, n.7.

11   See Chapter Twelve, 'Eucharist: Sacrificial Memorial and Sacred Banquet'.

CHAPTER SIX

Priests and People: Bound by Mutual Need

Apparent Tensions

Letters to Catholic publications and anecdotal evidence from other sources suggests that everything is not right with the relationship between priests and people in a number of parishes. There are complaints of unilateral and unexplained decision making and a suffocating insistence on insignificant rules. There are complaints that the personal preference of priests is substituted for magisterial teaching and that the theological disposition of parishioners is disregarded.

There are, of course, two parties to this tension, and it is usually only the laity who voice their complaints publicly. Priests tend to grumble among themselves. Both parties are often guilty of quoting magisterial teaching selectively without trying to gain a fuller understanding of its breadth and sophistication. A priest may argue that the Church is hierarchical and that he has every right to make whatever decisions he sees fit to make. How a hierarchy of service rather than power should operate is left unexplored. A parishioner may argue that the majority view of the congregation should determine how things are done. How discernment rather than democratic consensus informs decision-making is not considered.

A more holistic view of magisterial teaching on ordained ministry and the lay faithful should provide a way forward for both parties to the argument. Based on a reading of all the relevant documents on priesthood and laity since the turn of the twentieth century, this summary tries to capture the main themes and identify reasons why some interpretations of them go astray. Documents are indicated by abbreviations and section numbers in the text and listed below.

AA	*Apostolicam Actuositatem*, Conciliar Decree, 1965.
BXVI	General Audience, Pope Benedict XVI 2010.
CL	*Christifideles Laici* Apostolic Exhortation, Pope St John Paul II, 1988.
CNO	*On Certain Questions Regarding the Collaboration of the Non-Ordained Faithful in the Sacred Ministry of Priests*, Instruction, Joint Congregations, 1997.
CS	*Catholici Sacerdotii* Encyclical, Pope Pius XI, 1935.
DMLP	*Directory on the Ministry and Life of Priests*, Congregation for the Clergy, 1994.
F	Homily, Chrism mass, Pope Francis, 2013.
GPLA	*Guiding Principles of the Lay Apostolate*, Address, Pope Pius VII, 1957.
JPII	*Letter to Priests*, Pope St John Paul II, 1996.
LG	*Lumen Gentium*, Conciliar Dogmatic Constitution, 1964.
MN	*Menti Nostrae*, Apostolic Exhortation, Pope Pius XII, 1950.
MCC	*Mystici Corporis Christi*, Encyclical, Pope Pius XII, 1943.
PDV	*Pastores Dabo Vobis*, Apostolic Exhortation, Pope St John Paul II, 1992.
PL	*The Participation of the Laity in the Priestly Ministry*, Address, Pope St John Paul II, 1994.
PO	*Presbyterorum Ordinis*, Conciliar Degree, 1965.
PPL	*The Priest, Pastor and Leader of the Parish Community*, Congregation for the Clergy, 2002.
PTM	*The Priest and the Third Millennium: Teacher of the Word, Minister of the sacraments and Leader of the Community*, Congregation of the Clergy, 1999
VN	*Vehementer Nos*, Encyclical, Pope St Pius X, 1906.

The Ordained Before Vatican II

The teaching of the Catholic Church on priesthood can be seen to take its current shape at the Council of Trent in 1545. From this perspective priests are instituted to perpetuate Christ's sacrifice by saying Mass. Trent speaks of parishes being 'governed' by 'worthy and competent parish priests'. Indeed, priests are encouraged to lead blameless lives if they are to be able to correct the faults of lay people. During the seventeenth and eighteenth centuries priestly spirituality began to characterise ordination as effecting a change in the priest that linked him with the Eucharist in a special and personal way. As theologians began to argue that Christ's priesthood was intimately connected with his divinity, it became popular to regard priests as sharing in some mysterious way with this "highly mystical power."[1] On this basis, they were seen as having special spiritual powers and authority.

Late nineteenth and early twentieth century magisterial teaching continued to develop the themes already promulgated at Trent. Accordingly, priests are instruments in the hands of the Divine Redeemer (CS 12) and a continuation of Christ, having been sent out by the Father (12). Most significantly the priest makes Christ present on the altar and it is through this that the priest's "ineffable greatness" is shown (17). The priest dispenses the Sacraments through which "the grace of the Saviour floes for the good of humanity" (17). The priest is like 'another Christ' because he is marked with an indelible character making him, as it were, a living image of our Saviour. The priest has an important leadership role. He must guide consciences, comfort and sustain souls, and "fight error and repel vice" (MN 61). He betrays his calling if he is indulgent about "incorrect ways of thinking or acting". However, he must always be compassionate (ibid).

The Laity Before Vatican II

Unlike the priesthood, there is no developed theology of the laity prior to Vatican II. We must rely on occasional references within council and papal documents to determine the general attitude towards the laity, who are more generally referred to as 'the faithful' or simply 'the people'. The Council of Tent acknowledges that the laity are imprinted with a special character at baptism but is clear that they are the recipients of what Christ intended through the hierarchical structure of the Church.

The Church was judged to be an unequal society made up of two categories "the Pastors and the flock, those who occupy a rank in the different degrees of the hierarchy and the multitude of the faithful" (*VN* 8). Teaching and directing is the responsibility of the pastors and "the one duty of the multitude is to allow themselves to be led, and, like a docile flock, to follow the Pastors" (ibid). Because the laity are united with God in the Body of Christ, which is the Church, they have an "exalted supernatural nobility" (*MCC* 11). However, they are only regarded as occupying "an honourable, if often lowly, place in the Christian community" (17). They must revere their bishops as divinely appointed successors of the apostles (42) and "pay due honour and reverence to the more exalted members of the Mystical Body" (93).

The development of what became known as Catholic Action, where lay people tried to exert a Catholic influence on society was received with a mixed response from the *Magisterium*. The concept of the Lay Apostolate gathered momentum with the inauguration of the World Congress of the Lay Apostolate. However, this was seen as a participation in the apostolate of the hierarchy and subject to its authority. Lay people were allowed to be involved in a variety of ecclesial activities and this contribution to the work of the hierarchy was appreciated. However, their indispensable contribution was concerned with insinuating revealed truth into every aspect of life (GPLA 101) and in particular seeking social and economic justice for all people (112).

A Changing Context

The pre-Vatican II Church essentially saw itself as a hierarchical institution. Clearly at one level the Church is an institution as it has "stable organisational features."[2] However, Dulles is not alone in judging that the institution itself had become its own primary focus. Its hierarchical structure was exaggerated so that there was a clear division between those who taught, sanctified and governed and those who were in receipt of these ministrations. The Church was equated with the hierarchy, and the laity were lowly members, who were to be obedient to them. As St Pius X had taught, it was a Church of unequals.

Retrieving a much older tradition, the Vatican II Dogmatic Constitution on the Church, *Lumen Gentium*, teaches that all members of the Church share common attributes regardless of whether they are ordained or lay. Through baptism, all the people of God become members of "a chosen race, a royal priesthood, a holy nation, a people set apart…" (*LG* 9 cf. 1Pet 2:9–10). Sharing in the one priesthood of Christ, all the baptised are called to offer their entire lives as "a living sacrifice, holy and pleasing to God" (10). The priesthood of the ordained is seen as differing in "essence and degree" but also as being grounded in the same one priesthood of Christ as that shared by all the baptised. The ministerial priesthood exists in order to serve the priesthood of all believers (18). No longer were the laity to be considered second class citizens relying on the clergy for permission to fulfil the mission that was given to them by God at baptism.

The Laity After Vatican II

The full nature and dignity of the laity is brought into focus by Vatican II (cf. *CL* 2). There is no inequality between the People of God (*LG 32*), who share a common dignity, grace and vocation (ibid). The laity do not just belong to the Church but are the Church (*CL 9*). They are not only Christians but Christ himself (*CL* 17).

The laity are assigned their apostolate by Our Lord (*LG* 32) through baptism (*AA* 3). They are called to use their gifts in the Church and in the world (*AA* 5, *CL* 2). In the Church they may be called upon to assist the hierarchy. Their activities, which include active participation in the liturgy, proclamation of the Word and catechesis (*AA* 10, *CL* 2), are necessary if the work of the ordained is to be effective *(AA* 10). This is a manifestation of the "nature, dignity, spirituality, mission and responsibility" of lay people (*CL* 2). However, there is a danger that too much emphasis on their participation in the Church distracts them from their particular vocation to the world (*CL* 2).

The laity are called to make the divine message of salvation known (*AA* 3) and make Christ present in the world (*LG* 33). They are called to be holy (*LG* 39–42, *CL* 16), letting their witness to Christ penetrate and sanctify the world (*LG* 33, *AA* 13). In a sense it is this secular nature that sets the laity apart from the ordained (*CL* 15). It is not participation within the Church that is their special vocation but rather using their immersion in secular affairs to bring about renewal (*AA* 7). If they are to be effective witnesses, they must have a sound grasp of revealed truth and a well-formed conscience (*LG* 35).

The relationship between the ordained and the lay is one of mutual dependence. They are "bound to each other by mutual need" (*LG* 32). Vocations, ministries and charisms should be seen as complementary and not as conferring varying levels of dignity (*CL* 20). What distinguishes people is their capacity for service (ibid). The priests minister to the laity, providing spiritual sustenance. The laity assist, accept and obey their pastors (*LG* 37). However, the laity are sometimes obliged to express their opinions (ibid). Pastors for their part are to recognise and promote the dignity of the laity, allowing them to participate (ibid). Through this lay participation, the pastors themselves can be refreshed. The laity must treat their priests with filial love (*PO* 9) but they have a right and a duty to make their opinions known (PPL 26.2).

The Ordained After Vatican II

Despite sharing in the one priesthood of Christ with all the baptised faithful, the ordained participated in the priesthood of Christ in a different way (PPL 6.4 & 8.1). They are "configured to Christ" in a special way, which not only gives them a special role in "sanctifying, teaching and governing" (DMLP 6) but also links them in a unique way with Christ the high priest and shepherd (PL 4.7). Because of this special character, a priest acts with the authority of Christ and, particularly when he offers the eucharistic sacrifice, acts *in persona Christi capitis*, in the person of Christ the Head (JPII 1996). Through the priest, Christ's own actions are made present (BXVI 2010). As well as performing this important saving action, the priest teaches the truths necessary for salvation and cares for the people of God, leading them to sanctity (DMLP 7). The ordained are called to be a living witness to Christ, a sacramental representation, a faithful image of Christ the priests (DMLP 2).

Not only do the ordained represent Christ in a special way, but they are also intimately connected with the mystery of the Trinity. The Father is the ultimate origin of their power. He sends them forth and orientates them to His Kingdom. They are called by Christ and participate in the Son's redemptive mission. They are empowered and guided by the Holy Spirit through whom they exercise pastoral charity (cf. *PDV* & DMLP 4 & 20).

The qualities and virtues required by the ordained minister are demanding. They include faithfulness, integrity, wisdom and humility and also an ability to put the other person first (*PDV* 28). This will only be possible if they nurture their spiritual life through prayer and eucharistic devotion. They should study the Scriptures in the light of tradition and the teaching of the *Magisterium*, to whom they owe obedience. They must remain faithful to the teaching of the *Magisterium*, recognising that it is the Word of God that they share with others and not their own wisdom (DMLP 45). They must avoid reducing or diluting the message even if they find some of it difficult to accept (PTM ch4, 3). In particular, they must not distort the message (DMLP 45) or use their preaching in pursuit of their own objectives (PTM ch2, 1).

If they are able to live up to their calling then they will be a herald of hope (DMLP 35), a font of life and vitality for the parish (PPL 8) and an incomparable force for the progress of the entire world (DMLP conc. 4). As "fathers in Christ" (*LG* 28) they are to "take care of the faithful" by being an example to them. They are to lead and serve them in such a way that they are worthy to be called the Church of God (*LG* 28).

Priests and People

The priests seek "the glory of God resplendent in his people, alive and strengthened" (F 2013). Recognising the dignity of the laity as children of God (*PDV* 17), priests should value their God-given gifts and encourage co-responsibility with them (*PDV* 30). The ministries, offices and roles of the laity, which have their origin in baptism and confirmation, should be acknowledged and fostered (PPL 24.2). Priests must listen to lay people, give brotherly consideration to their wishes, mindful that the Holy Spirit informs their intuitions (CNO A22) and recognising their experience and competence (*PO* 9). Priests must try to reconcile differences so that no one feels a stranger in the community (*PO* 9) or that they are treated with indifference (DMLP 36).

The priest's authority comes from Christ and so does his dedication to service (*PDV* 21). He must set aside all attitudes of superiority or of exercising power over people (*PDV* 58). Authority is to be exercised in humble and authoritative service (DMLP 16). Oppressive domination must not characterise his ministry but rather a willingness to serve (PTM ch4, 3), remembering that priesthood does not itself signify a greater degree of holiness (CNO 1). Advising against authoritarianism, the *Magisterium* also warns against democratisation. The priest must take the lead, but that leadership must be sensitive, collaborative and inclusive, recognising that the priest is "in" the Church as well as "in front of" it. "He is a brother among brothers" [sic] (*PDV* 74). He must become a bridge and not an obstacle for others in their meeting with Jesus Christ (*PDV* 43).

Getting the balance right will not always be easy. The divine origin of the priestly vocation and its special relationship to Christ and the Trinity must not deceive the ordained into believing that 'Father knows best'. The common or royal priesthood of all the baptised and the intuition for the faith granted to them through the power of the Holy Spirit must not lead the laity to expect fully democratic decision making. What is required is mutual respect and charitable reciprocity informed by the unabridged teaching of the *Magisterium*.

Endnotes

1 McBrien, *Catholicism*, p. 872.
2 A. Dulles, *Models of the Church*, (Dublin: Gill & Macmillan, 1988), p. 34.

CHAPTER SEVEN

Lay Ministry: A Developing and Growing Reality

Introduction

One consequence of the shortage of priests has been an acknowledgement that lay people will have to play a fuller part in the life of the Church. Increasingly, lay ministry is encouraged and advocated as a positive response that resonates clearly with the teaching of Vatican II. However, within the Catholic Church there seems to be a reluctance to use the term 'ministry' when referring to the work of the laity, preferring to call it function or apostolate, and a preference for reserving 'ministry' as a description of the work of those who are ordained. There would appear to be a degree of ambiguity in magisterial teaching on lay ministry.

Ministry: A Disputed Term

Some of the ambiguity is a result of different ways of interpreting ministry as it appears in the New Testament. The word that is used in Greek is *diakonia*, which can be taken to mean 'humble service' or 'authoritative stewardship'. Those who understand *diakonia* in terms of humble service consider it to be "lowly and costly love of one's neighbour",[1] and "an activity which every Greek would recognise at once as being one of self-abasement".[2] Those who see it as authoritative stewardship argue that in Greek literature *diakonia* does not imply humble service or self-denial but rather identifies someone who acts as an agent for a higher authority.[3]

Another dispute over the meaning of *diakonia* in the New Testament concerns the extent to which the ministry that it implies is general or specific. If ministry is one of those many ways of serving that are referred to by St Paul (cf. 1 Cor 12:4–6) and arise from the gifts that we all receive from the Spirit (I Cor 7:7), then it can be argued that all the baptised are called to ministry. An alternative perspective sees the gifts that are freely given by the Spirit empowering all the baptised to serve the community, but before this service becomes ministry it requires designation by a commissioning person or institution. It has been argued that St Paul considers being *diakonos* (one having a ministry) of God as more important than being an apostle.

In many ways the question raised by these two interpretations remain with us today and influence Church teaching. One of the protagonists in this debate, John Collins, formulates the question succinctly: "is ministry a baptismal charism, and thus an inherent capacity of any Christian, or is it a pastoral function restricted to those who are ordained?"

Ministry and Service

In English, *diakonia* is typically translated as ministry or service. The different connotations of service and ministry, when they are used colloquially, fuels the dispute. It can be argued that all ministry is service but not all service is ministry. Service, from the Latin *servitium*, has its origins in lowly service, slavery and servitude. In English it is used in many varied contexts. People take their car in for a service, attend a religious service, sign up for military service or avail themselves of customer service in a shop. People who worked 'below stairs' in great households were said to be 'in service'. Most commonly, 'service' was associated with attendance during a meal. Public utilities such as transport, communications, electricity and water are regarded as services. Essentially. service is concerned with helping or doing work for someone other than yourself.

Generally, ministry is not associate with many of these types of service. Ministry is not how one would describe the service provided by car mechanics, bus drivers, electrical engineers or military personnel. Ministry is associate with doing things for others but, even then, the casual assistance offered to a neighbour would not be regarded as ministry. It would appear that service only becomes ministry when other conditions are also met.

Turning Service into Ministry

What might these conditions be? Casual assistance does not count as ministry but a regular commitment to assistance may do so. Someone who does not really know how to provide particular assistance may do more harm than good and would only be regarded as exercising a ministry if they had been properly trained to perform the tasks that they undertook. Although someone who has appropriate training and commitment may be commended for offering a service, it is unlikely to be regarded as a ministry by others unless they are acting on behalf of some recognised body. Ministry begins to emerge from general service by requiring regular commitment, training and authorisation.

Entry into Christian ministry is through baptism, by which one is called to discipleship of Jesus Christ and incorporated into his priestly, prophetic and kingly mission. Every individual comes to the Church with specific gifts and talents and is expected to use these for the building up of the Kingdom of God. Through baptism, all are called to service, but before this service can be called ministry, it needs those other attributes of training, commitment and authorisation. Consequently, those who are asked to become extraordinary ministers of Holy Communion, or readers or servers are expected to undertake training and be commissioned for their task. Some are called to take on additional responsibilities within the community as deacons, priests and bishops. Their training is longer, their commitment lifelong, and their initiation into the ministry is marked by sacramental ordination.

What is Christian Ministry?

It has been pointed out that many scholars have described ministry, but few have defined it. A definition that resonates with my own reading of ministry is offered by Thomas O'Meara. Ministry is "the public activity of a baptised follower of Jesus Christ flowing from the Spirit's charism and an individual personality on behalf of a Christian community to witness to, serve and realise the kingdom of God."[4]

O'Meara sees ministry as something active. It involves doing something, not just being someone. I may be an Extraordinary Minister of Holy Communion but if I never distribute Communion, then I am not exercising my ministry. The activity is performed on behalf of the Christian community not in order to enhance my own standing but because it needs to be done and I am able to do it. It is a gift (charism) that is received from the Holy Spirit by someone who is a sacramentally initiated member of the community and who may also be ordained. A ministry has its own identity and limits to its scope, which locate it within a variety of actions that are regarded as ministry. Not all acts of service are ministry. It is public not private action, although it may be discreet. Critically, the action takes Christ as its inspiration and is undertaken for the sake of the Kingdom of God.

The Development of Ministry

The more charismatic communities and those with a variety of different ministerial structures that we find in the New Testament may represent an experimental stage in the development of ministry in the Church. Whether internal and external pressures required a more uniform system is a matter of speculation amongst scholars. By the third century a structure involving a single *episkapos*/bishop with a group of *prebyteroi*/pastors and *diakonoi*/deacons became the norm. These three ministries would eventually emerge as the bishops, priests and deacons with which we are familiar today. It seems likely that they would have been commissioned in some way, most probably by the laying on of hands. Although they exercised specific functions within the community, there is no evidence that they saw themselves as separated from the rest of the faithful. There was no distinction between clerics and lay because the designations did not exist.

Clerical and Lay an Ahistoric Distinction

'Clerical' comes from the Greek *Kleros (κλῆρος)*, which means 'lot', as in Acts 1:26 where a replacement for Judas is chosen by drawing lots and the "lot fell on Matthias". *Kleros* was first used to identify a particular group of officials in the 'Apostolic Tradition of Hippolytus', written about AD 215. Such a group is not identified in the New Testament and where 1 Peter 5:3 uses the word *Kleros*, it refers to all the people, those who have been chosen for the eschatological Kingdom (the fulness of God's Kingdom at the end of time). Laity is not a description used in Scripture, but *Laos* is, and *Laos* means the people as in 'God's people' as distinct from the Gentiles.[5]

Ministry Becomes Clericalised

Gradually, those in a clerical state grew further apart from their lay brethren. The development of the monastic system during the early Middle Ages encouraged a belief that only through a life divorced from the ordinary could true holiness be attained. By the ninth century, priests were being encouraged to adopt a lifestyle similar to that of the monks. In the monasteries, the leader had significant authority and this, together with the ubiquitous, hierarchical feudal system, through which ordinary people's lives were governed, reinforced the relative status of members of the Church. The distance between people and priests was growing.

During the Middle Ages, and particularly under the Christian kings and emperors in Europe, the bishops became important national figures and often held high offices of state. Power structures of hierarchy were the norm. The priests were better educated than most of the people and were increasingly regarded as set apart.

The Middle Ages, influenced as it was by a philosophical system (Neoplatonism) that conceived reality as hierarchical, also saw the distinction made between the clerical and the lay states of life. The *ordo clericorum*, who were dedicated to the spiritual realm was a higher state than the *ordo laicorum*, who were concerned with the material world. A dualism between the sacred and profane is present here, with the ordained concerned with the sacred and the lay with the mundane.[6] By the end of the eleventh century priests were seen as exercising a 'sacred power', associated with their unique role in celebrating the Eucharist rather than having a ministry of service to the community. As the Church entered the twentieth century, the distinction between the ordained and the lay was accepted as "instituted by Christ"[7] although the historical evidence for this is elusive.[8]

Ministry Retrieved from The Clerical State

Despite the retrieval of the common or royal priesthood of all the baptised at Vatican II, and magisterial efforts to emphasise the collaborative role of the entire people of God, ministry in the Catholic Church is generally associated with those who hold an office in the Church, particularly the ordained.

Everyone may be called to service, it would seem, but not all are called to ministry. Commonly, ministry is associated with liturgical and ecclesial action, and beyond these activities the work of the laity is seen as their apostolate. In *Sacrosanctum Concilium* (the Vatican II Constitution on the Sacred Liturgy), ministry is mainly associated with the ordained or with those fulfilling a liturgical function such as servers, lectors, commentators, and members of the choir.[9]

Ambiguity in Magisterial Teaching on Ministry

However, there is a lack of consistency in the use of this terminology and a widespread use of the word ministry to describe many activities undertaken by the nonordained. Pope Paul VI sees the laity exercising "different kinds of ministries according to the grace and charisms which the Lord has been pleased to bestow on them".[10] A joint instruction from eight curial departments recognised the call for the people of God to participate in the mission of the church "through the dynamic of an organic communion in accord with their diverse ministries and charisms".[11] In this way the laity continue the mission and ministry of Christ, who is the source of all ministry. However, the instruction also asserts that the designation ministry only assumes its full meaning when attributed to the ordained. The instruction acknowledges 'functions' that belong to the lay faithful but argues that the term 'ministry' only applies to those 'offices' that have been delegated by the Church.

In his exhortation on the Lay faithful, *Christifideles Laici*, Pope St John Paul II makes a clear distinction between the ordained and the lay faithful but stresses that there must be respect for "the other ministries, offices and roles in the Church, which are rooted in the Sacraments of Baptism and Confirmation".[12] In his Encyclical *Novo Millennio Ineunte*, he alludes to a more diverse range of ministries, which may be "formally instituted or simply recognised". He sees the flourishing of such ministries as good for the whole community "sustaining it in all its many needs". He identifies among these needs not only catechesis and liturgy but also "education of the young" and "charitable works".[13]

General and Particular Ministry

Given academic disputes regarding the nature of Christian ministry and the apparent ambiguity of Church teaching, what are we to make of lay ministry? In seeking a better understanding of what is meant by 'ministry', it is possible to consult the document from the Catholic Bishops Conference of England and Wales (CBCEW) on collaborative ministry called 'The Sign We Give'. In this, the bishops recognise that the term 'ministry' has been subject to considerable pastoral and theological reflection since Vatican II and that it is not easy to define.

Avoiding the complexity of the debate surrounding the term ministry, the CBCEW offer two insights, which are of particular help in the present discussion. Firstly "ministry is rightly understood as the service based on baptism and confirmation to which all are called."[14] In other words, it belongs to those who are "fully initiated members of the Church."[15] Ministry is the way that the baptised express their discipleship in various areas of their life.

Secondly, the bishops use the term ministry in reference to "particular roles or actions to which individuals are called by the Church and which they carry out for and on behalf of the whole body." Among these they specify extraordinary ministers of Holy Communion, catechists and readers, and also teachers.[16]

Lay Ecclesial Ministry

The Bishops make a clear distinction between ordained ministry and unordained ministry. Writing ten years later, the United States Conference of Catholic Bishops (USCCB) follow Pope St John Paul II in asserting that the main focus of the lay ministry is secular.[17] They are concerned with insinuating the Christian worldview into the culture of their day. However, the USCCB also accept that the laity serve in various ministries, offices and roles which do not require ordination but have their foundation in the Sacraments of

Initiation and Matrimony. The USCCB use the term 'lay ecclesial ministers' to describe a number of possible roles but make it clear that this is not the name for a specific position. They do however acknowledge that it represents a "developing and growing reality".[18]

Conclusion

There is little doubt that all the baptised are called to *diakonia* understood as service, but ministry is more accurately used to identify roles that involve training, commitment and designation by the Church. Given these conditions, lay ministry is a legitimate term and one with which we will no doubt become more familiar.

Endnotes

1   W. Brandt, *Dienst und Dienen im Neuen Testament*, (Giltersloh: Bertelsmann, 1931), Quoted in J.N. Collins, 'Ordained and other Ministries: making a Difference', *Ecclesiology* 3.1 (2006), 11–32, Sage Publications, p. 15.

2   H. Küng, *The Church*, (New York: Image Books, 1976), p. 498. English Translation of original 1967 edition.

3   Cf. J.N. Collins, *Diakonia Studies: Critical Issues in Ministry*, (Oxford & New York: Oxford University Press, 2014).

4   T.F. O'Meara, *Theology of Ministry*, (New York: Paulist Press, 1999), p. 150.

5   *Laos* also conveys the meaning 'populace' or 'general public'.

6   Cf. S.K. Wood, *Sacramental Orders*, (Minnesota: Liturgical Press, 2000), p. 23.

7   1917 Code of Canon Law, canon 107.

8   K. Osborne, *Ministry: Lay Ministry in the Roman Catholic Church* (New York: Paulist Press, 1993), pp. 41–44.

9   Cf. Pope Paul VI *Sacrosanctum Concilium*, (Vatican Website 1963)[*SC*], n. 29.

10   Pope Paul VI, *Evangelii Nuntiandi* (Vatican Website, 1975) [*EN*], n. 73.

11   Interdicasterial Instruction on Certain Questions Regarding the Collaboration of the Non-ordained Faithful in the Sacred Ministry of Priests, *Ecclesiae de Mysterio*, (Vatican City, 1997), Premise.

12 *CL*, n. 23.
13 Pope St John Paul II, *Novo Millennio Ineunte* (Vatican Website, 2001), n. 46.
14 CBCEW, *The Sign We Give*, (Essex: Matthew James Publishing, 1995), p. 18.
15 ibid., p. 10.
16 ibid., p. 18.
17 Cf. *CL*, n.15.
18 USCCB, *Co-workers in the Vineyard of the Lord*, (www.usccb.org. 2005).

CHAPTER EIGHT

Teaching as Ministry

Called to Ministry

Catholic teachers are called to ministry by the whole Church on whose behalf they act. This is frequently recognised by services of dedication at the beginning of a new school year or when a new headteacher is appointed. The teachers commit themselves to serving the community where they work and ask for God's help in their ministry. On behalf of the Church, a priest often commissions them to fulfil this role. Given the new understanding of ministry arising from Vatican II and recognising that these lay teachers share in the one priesthood of Christ, it should be recognised that it is Christ who calls them and sends them to do his work, and the hierarchy of the Church acknowledges this. Rather in the way that two people give the sacrament of matrimony to each other in the presence of a priest, the teachers accept their God-given ministry in the presence of a priest.

Teaching in Scripture

There are many references to teachers (διδασκάλους) in the New Testament, and it is the same word used by earlier Greek writers such as Plato. It is a word that has an enduring and unambiguous meaning. Teachers facilitate learning however they go about it.

Jesus was recognised as a teacher because of the miracles that he worked and the signs that he gave (Jn 3:2). This was a designation that he readily accepted (Jn 13:13). He taught with authority (Matt 7:29) and was not influenced by the status of those who heard him but remained faithful to the Gospel he had come to proclaim (Mk 12:14).

Although St Paul thought that everyone shared some responsibility for teaching (Col 3:16), he also recognises teaching as a particular charism. Teachers did not choose the role for themselves and were not selected by the community but received their commission from God (1 Cor 12:28; Eph 4:11-13; Acts 13:1). As a charism, a gift of the Spirit, it may be that teachers had hands laid on them by the elders of the community as was the case with Timothy (1Tim 4:14). Unlike Timothy, however, most teachers were not itinerant preachers but were members of a definite community where they carried out their ministry.

Teachers are called to help God's people come to perfection so that they can work together to build up the body of Christ (Eph 4:12). They are teaching the Good News of Jesus Christ, "declaring the whole of God's purpose" (Acts 20:27), passing on what they themselves have heard (2 Tim 2:2). A good knowledge of Scripture is required if a teacher is to help others understand its implications for their lives (Lk 24:13-35; Acts 8:29-35; Acts 28:23-24). All Scripture is important and is required in order to teach doctrine, correct errors and guide people's lives (2 Tim 3:16). This knowledge, in the hands of a skilful teacher, may even set the pupils' hearts on fire (Lk 24:32). People are to be taught to put their trust in the living God, who is the Saviour of the world (1Tim 4:10).

Teachers must understand what they teach and not offer empty speculations like the teachers of the Law (1 Tim 1:6-7). As the body of Christ is built up and a unity in faith is established, then people will no longer be misled by misguided or unscrupulous teachings (Eph 4:9-16). A teacher helps people to be resistant to such teachings.

Characteristics of An Effective Teacher

In order to be effective, teachers must speak with authority (Titus 2:15 also see Matt 5:19) and remember that it is not their own wisdom that they are sharing but God's (1 Cor 1:10-31). Teachers also have to judge whether people require "milk" or "meat", elementary teaching or more sophisticated doctrine. Indeed, it may be that there is a regular need to return to the basics (Heb 5:12-14, 6:1-3).

Teachers must be reliable (2 Tim 2:2) and set a good example by keeping God's commandments and never suggesting that these commandments should be ignored (Rom 2:21-23; Matt 5:19). By their "integrity, dignity and sound speech" they must provide no grounds for criticism that their opponents can use against them (Titus 2:7-8). They must have a generous disposition and be joyful because of the hope that is in them, resolute in times of difficulty, prayerful, charitable and hospitable (Rom 12:3-13).

Only One Teacher

The theologian, Clare Watkins, points out that from the time of the apostles onward, teaching has played an important part in the growth of the Church and in spreading the Gospel. The Church holds its most significant teachers in high esteem designating them as doctors of the Church. Down to the present day, some religious orders recognise teaching as their major charism and the Vatican has a congregation dedicated to Catholic education. However, Jesus told his disciples that they should not allow themselves to be called teachers as there is only one teacher and that is Christ himself (Matt 23:8-10). Reflecting on this, Tertullian argued that it was always the Holy Spirit who teaches. Thomas Aquinas argued that it was possible to shine a light on the one teaching of Jesus Christ. The tradition of the Church implies that teachers pass on a teaching that is not their own. They participate in the teaching ministry of Christ.[1]

The Sacramental Nature of Ministry

Catholics are said to have a sacramental imagination.[2] It is called an imagination because it is not confined by the empirically verifiable but imagines possibilities that go beyond these. It is sacramental because it recognises the imprint of God on all created things. A sacrament is an outward sign of something divine that is hidden. Catholics use their imagination to transcend the mundane. They recognise that the words that they use in relation to God are inadequate and that they have to be regarded as analogical,[3] being simultaneously similar and dissimilar. For example, Catholics know that they are not describing God when they say that God is three and one but rather, they are using their imagination to try and reveal something about God which is beyond their experience. A sacramental imagination opens up new possibilities. It sets reality within a richer context, which is not just theoretical but essentially existential.

All Christian ministry is modelled on that of Jesus Christ. As the catechism says, "Christ is himself the source of ministry in the Church".[4] All ministry in the Church originates in Jesus Christ. Ministers are, in a sense, sent out by him as the apostles were. In fact, the original Hebrew word *Shalah*, translated into Greek as *apostello*, means 'to send out with the authority of the sender'. All the ministries undertaken by the Christian community and by individual Christians are a sign or sacrament of the ministry of Jesus Christ.

Icons of Christ

In modelling themselves on Jesus Christ and embracing his mission—recognising that they have been 'sent out' by him—teachers accept the role as signs or sacraments of his presence among his people. Ministry is to be found at the point where the human and the divine converge or, as O'Meara puts it, "at the invisible horizon where grace seeks to become concrete in the world…"[5] Rather like Icons that in the Eastern Christian tradition represent a window on the supernatural and encourage us to look beyond and behind what we experience with our senses to what we perceive through faith, ministry points beyond the person engaged in ministry to Christ himself.

Sacramental Perspective

This sacramental perspective gives ministry its particular Christological focus. It allowed Archbishop (now Cardinal) Vincent Nichols to argue that acceptance of the centrality of Jesus Christ in the life of the school is a crucial requirement for those who lead Catholic schools. "Faith in Jesus Christ and faith in the outflow of that presence of Christ into the Church is the key component to effective leadership in a Catholic school."[6] Further, he argues that nurture and practice within the Catholic community produces leaders who are guided by a Catholic vision of reality, which sees a world created by God, redeemed by Christ and transformed by the Holy Spirit. This is clearly an expectation and acknowledgement of the sacramental perspective at work in the schools.

The Congregation for Catholic Education (CCE) tells us that "Christ is the foundation of the whole educational enterprise in a Catholic school."[7] Christ is at the centre of the school, but it is the sharing of this Christ-centred vision that makes the school distinctively Catholic.

Teachers teach the Christian message in words and deeds, by their formal instruction of the pupils and by the example that they give. Pope Paul VI sums up the importance of this teaching by example when he asserts that "modern man listens more willingly to witnesses than to teachers, and if he does listen to teachers, it is because they are witnesses."[8] The CCE take up the importance of witness asserting that "conduct is always much more important than speech. Students should see in their teachers the Christian attitude and behaviour that is often so conspicuously absent from the secular atmosphere in which they live."[9] Again, four years later, the CCE teaches that the "prime responsibility for creating this unique Christian school climate rests with the teachers, as individuals and as a community."[10] In all these examples the teacher is called upon to be a sign of the centrality of Jesus Christ in our schools. There can be little doubt that this sacramental perspective, with which a largely secular society is neither familiar nor comfortable,[11] allows Catholics to offer an educational vision that acknowledges the presence of the divine.

Collaborative Ministry

Ministry is not only sacramental, but it is also collaborative. It is not something that is done by an individual on their own initiative. It is an action on behalf of the whole Christian community. It is distinctive, yet one of a plethora of interrelated actions. It is not random or chaotic but coordinated and intended. Ministry is, by its very nature, collaborative, and finds its theological justification within the Trinity. Catholics are familiar with what remains a profound mystery. God is one and God is three. Tertullian (AD 155–225) was the first to use the terms 'substance' and 'persons' in a legal sense of a property and an individual with the right to hold property, paving the way for a belief in three persons and one substance.[12] The Council of Nicaea (AD 325) that formulated the creed most regularly used in Catholic churches acknowledged that there was One and Three but it did not offer an explanation of the relationship between them.

God Exists as Relationship

The Church's understanding of this mystery has developed over time, and for many centuries was concerned with philosophical distinctions. In trying to encapsulate what could be gleaned from Scripture, attempts were made to distinguish the roles within the Trinity without compromising its unity. Accordingly, the Father generates, the Son was begotten, and the Spirit proceeded.[13] This can appear to create an unhelpful hierarchy within the Godhead. Following the Cappadocian Fathers in the fourth century,[14] the Catholic doctrine rejects any subordination. "Each of the persons is that supreme reality" the catechism teaches. "God is one but not solitary". It is the relationship between the persons of the Trinity that is the real distinction between them. The orthodox priest (now Metropolitan) and scholar John Zizioulas has argued that we should not try and understand God in terms of persons and substance but in terms of relationship because God only exists as relationship.[15]

We are made in the image of God and so we can only really be understood in relationship to others. After all, it is only through relationship with God and other people that our sense of self develops. Our relationships are not incidental to our lives. They are formative and give individual lives meaning and purpose. Nurturing relationships is an important prerequisite for living the Christian life. The individual only becomes truly a person within a network of relationships that we call a community.

Collaboration and Communion

Collaborative ministry grows out of the Church seen as communion, a relationship between people and between people and their God. The report of the working party into collaborative ministry on behalf of the CBCEW describes collaborative ministry in a number of ways. We are called to be a "company of disciples" engaged in a "mutual process of conversion and formation." Individual gifts and vocations should be expressed fully. They are "complementary and mutually enriching."[16]

In a passage that could be just as much about leadership in schools as leadership in the Church, the bishops say that it is through the quality of relationships that leaders invite people to make full use of their gifts and energy and that it is only by letting go of responsibilities and trusting others that the "interconnection of relationships"[17] required for communion will develop. Where people are expected to be submissive, their creativity is supressed, and their contribution minimised.[18]

Collaborative ministry requires both psychological and spiritual maturity. It requires a willingness to share power and influence. It requires humility. All of which are countercultural characteristics within our competitive society. More autocratic leaders can sometimes appear collaborative and indeed may well consider themselves to be collaborative. In truth, however, they only allow people to work for them rather than with them.

Conclusion

All ministry in the Church is modelled on the ministry of Christ of whom the teacher is a sign or sacrament. Ministry is collaborative, taking its inspiration from the Trinity and recognising that the body of Christ is made up of people who all have God-given gifts required for the building of the Kingdom.

Teaching has always been an important ministry in the Church, and teachers can regard their ministry as given to them by God and authorised by the Church.

Endnotes

1   Cf. C. Watkins, 'Discovering a Theology for the Christian Teacher Today' in *Journal of Education and Christian Belief*, 12.1 (2008), 53–68, pp. 55/56.

2   A. Greeley, *The Catholic Imagination*, (Berkeley and London: University of California Press, 2000).

3   Cf. D. Tracey, 'The Catholic Analogical Imagination' Presidential Address: Catholic Theological Society of America, (1977). http://ejournals.bc.edu/ojs/index.php/ctsa/article/view/2887/2512. D. Tracey, *The Analogical Imagination: Christian Theology and the Culture of Pluralism*, (SCM-Canterbury Press, 1981).

4   CCC, n. 874.

5   O'Meara, *Theology of Ministry*, p. 229.

6   V. Nichols, *Leading a Catholic School*, speaking at a conference jointly hosted by the CES and Heythrop Institute for Religion, Ethics and Public Life, entitled 'Visions for Leadership', March 2009.

7   CCE, *The Catholic School*, n. 34.

8   *EN*, n.41.

9   CCE, *Lay Catholics in Schools*, n.32.

10   CCE, *The Religious Dimension of Education in A Catholic School: Guidelines for Reflection and Renewal*, (London: CTS, 1988), n. 26.

11   G. Muller, *Priesthood and Diaconate*, (San Francisco, Ignatius Press, 2002), p. 32.

12   For passages from Tertullian's thesis Against Praxeus, see H. Bettenson (ed.), *The early Christian Fathers*, (Oxford University Press, Oxford, 1956), pp. 133-137.

13   CCC, n. 254.

14   Basil the Great (330-379), who was bishop of Caesarea; Basil's younger brother Gregory of Nyssa (c.332-395), who was bishop of Nyssa; and a close friend, Gregory of Nazianzus (329-389), who became Patriarch of Constantinople.

15   J.D. Zizioulas, *Being as Communion*, (Longman Todd, 1985).

16   Cf. CBCEW, *The Sign We Give* (Essex: Matthew James Publishing, 1995), p. 20.

17   Pope St John Paul II, *Pastores Dabo Vobis* (Vatican website, 1992), n. 12.

18   Cf. CBCEW, *The Sign We Give*, p. 23.

CHAPTER NINE

A Catholic Curriculum

Education: Differing Perspectives

Albert Einstein remarked that "education is what you have left when you have forgotten everything you learned in school." Among the things left when you have forgotten what you learnt at school must surely be feelings, intuitions, the way that you perceive things, how you interpret your experiences, how to relate to other people, your capacity to learn new things, your imagination, sense of mystery and the wonder of creation.

I attended a conference on 'The Changing School: A Challenge to the Teacher' in the early 1970s and was treated to a talk by Sir Alec Clegg, who at the time was the Education Officer for the West Riding of Yorkshire. Among other things he used a phrase that has remained with me throughout my career. It appeared in any prospectus that I wrote and, in many ways, serves as an anthem for Catholic education. He said simply that "the person the child is becoming is more important than what he or she knows".

We need faith, hope and love if we are to live life to the full. If we are to develop a sense of mystery and give meaning to our lives, if we are to embrace a vision without which we will perish, then we require more than facts and figures.[1] It is this 'more than' that allows us to become fully human.

There is a concern among educationalists that the school curriculum, which once embraced this expansive vision of education, a vision that allowed John Dewey to refer to the teacher as "the usherer in of the Kingdom of God",[2] has become something much narrower. Within the modern educational framework, values have to be measurable, aims have to be written as observable targets, and education itself can be characterised as a means to noneducational ends such as grades and jobs.[3] In a sense, schools are no longer offering 'education as formation', as something intrinsically worthwhile, but rather 'education as preparation', as an extrinsic utility.

Catholic Curriculum

In the middle of the nineteenth century, before the Foster Act of 1870, there was a Catholic curriculum in terms of what was actually taught. "Hymns were used in singing lessons, Catholic scriptures provided reading material, St Paul's journeys the topics for geography and the lives of the saints for history lessons."[4] These days are gone. We make no claim that there is a 'Catholic' mathematics or science or technology. We don't suggest that there is a 'Catholic' way of learning history or geography, although we may interpret history and the progress of peoples from a Catholic perspective. We may try to help our students see all knowledge as a window on the divine, but this relies heavily of the individual teacher's own sacramental imagination.

Surely a Catholic curriculum is a 'total curriculum' which has a lasting influence on our pupils—something that remains when all that they learnt at school has been forgotten. If we are to provide this, then we must recognise that the philosophy that underpins our provision—often encapsulated by what we call ethos—has to be coherent and explicit. A coherent philosophy of education has to be built on a coherent philosophy of life because "if life lacks a sense of direction, so will the education it is possible to give our children."[5]

The person the child is becoming will be influenced significantly by the dominant philosophy of the school that they attend and that in turn will be shaped by the values and attitudes, one might say the *zeitgeist*, of the society within which it resides. If there is to be a Catholic curriculum, then a Catholic worldview must permeate the whole life of the school including its pedagogy. Indeed, this is one of the main justifications for Catholic schools.

Some see the coherent pre-Vatican II philosophy of education, upon which the initial consensus on Catholic schools was built, threatened by a failure to articulate an all embracing post-conciliar philosophy of education. It is argued that Catholic bishops have paid too little attention to a coherent holistic Catholic approach to education whilst accepting pragmatic and incompatible responses from Catholic schools to the changing national educational environment.[6] Others acknowledge diversification within a previously more homogenous Catholic system but see this as reflecting the greater openness encouraged by Vatican II.[7]

Philosophical Tensions

That there are tensions between dominant cultural assumptions and a Catholic way of seeing the world is indisputable.[8] The extent to which we recognise and manage these tensions will have a profound influence on the extent to which we can claim to be delivering a Catholic curriculum.

This, then, is where we come to critical tensions that exists within our Catholic schools. These are many and varied but here are some examples.

First, there is an anthropological tension. Our society considers us to be autonomous individuals who are self-made and should be free to live life as we choose during our short lifespan. Christians believe that we are an indebted people, created by God, redeemed by Christ and destined for everlasting life. It is only when we acknowledge our dependence on the grace (love) of God that we are able to make the most of our lives.

Second, there is a tension over the meaning of truth. Paradoxically, our society understands truth as either correspondence with verifiable empirical data or as whatever an individual perceives it to be. Christians believe that Jesus Christ is the truth, and the closer we align our lives with his the closer to the truth we come. As we come to understand that truth is a person, we discern the objective and contingent nature of truth, a truth towards which we are striving through a life lived with integrity, but a truth that is always approximate and inevitably just beyond our reach.

Third, there is a tension over the social nature of the human person. Our society is increasingly individualistic. We are told, and indeed teachers often tell their students, that it is possible to become all that we are able to become as a result of our own efforts. Christians understand the relational nature of God and the Church and recognise that human flourishing depends on community. Indeed, we only develop as a person in relation to other people.

Fourth, there is a tension over the purpose of education. In our society the purpose of education is competence, and its currency is diligence. We tell our students that they need good grades to be successful in life and to achieve these grades they must work hard. Christians see education as leading to maturity and the currency is love (cf. Eph 4:11–16). Education is concerned with a journey that has its end in the warm embrace of a loving God. Love is an antidote to pride and selfishness and a prerequisite for embracing the needs of other people. This growing maturity brings us closer to Christ himself.

Practical Tensions

For education, these tensions can be expressed as a number of questions that Catholic educationalists must ask themselves. The first four are interrelated. First, is our focus on average performance across the school or the progress and achievement of each individual child? The personal attributes and circumstances of individuals can be overlooked when hidden within the statistics for the whole school. What matters to the teacher is not impersonal statistical data but how particular students performed and what that means for their future hopes and dreams. In many cases, striving to achieve national standards is not in tension with our concern with the individual. If the individuals do well, so does the school. But what if that individual's needs are less about academic success and more a need for emotional support?

Second, is our goal efficiency and success at all costs? Do we teach to the test or are we committed to delivering an integral education which balances the demands for intellectual, emotional, physical, social and spiritual education? Can we find time for retreats and Masses or are they regarded as a distraction from the important task of improving results? How much is our curriculum skewed towards core subjects and away from the arts, humanities and religious education?

Third, do targets lead to an emphasis on the greatest good of the greatest number? Is this utilitarian approach in tension with our concern for the dignity of the individual, which in turn promotes the common good i.e. the good of all not just the majority. How do we demonstrate our commitment to those who Pope Francis describes as being on the margins? Are their interests ever sacrificed for the sake of the majority?

Fourth, are the mantras we use to motivate our students underpinned by a genuinely moral purpose? Competition, which is the hallmark of a market driven education, encourages self-interest and the pursuit of excellence for personal gain. Catholic schools claim to promote excellence in order to enable a greater level of service in solidarity with other people. Are we sure that our students understand this distinction or is the strength of our encouragement too heavily weighted towards personal success and what that will mean to the individual?

Fifth, is promoting British values synonymous with developing Christian or Gospel values? Interest in teaching 'British values' as a response to a perceived erosion of national identity due to immigration led to much debate about what they might be. The DfE identifies them as democracy, the rule of law, individual liberty and mutual respect and tolerance of those with different faiths and beliefs. There is no tension between these values and Catholic teaching, but Catholic education goes further. By assimilating an ethical code, students are able to make judgements about the value of what they learn and how best to make use of it. In a sense, British values are external; they provide a framework for community living. Moral values are internal; they shape the way that we live and influence how we perceive the world.

Sixth, do we reinforce non-judgemental pluralism, which is the hallmark of secular humanism. Do our schools implicitly accept that no lifestyle, values or system of belief is superior to another. Those who accept this assertion claim that we should not presume to judge between them. They argue that as long as I do not harm other people (although what constitutes harm is disputed), my views and perceptions are as valid as those of anyone else. For Catholics, Jesus' humanity is the reference point for all that is fully human. This provides us with a point of comparison with which to judge our own actions and those of others. Uncomfortable as it may be for many teachers, we believe that Jesus Christ is the fullness of God's revelation to humanity and it is through our relationship with him that we learn the truth about what it means to be fully human.

Conclusion

I am not implying that Catholic schools do not operate on the basis of a coherent philosophy of education which reflects a Catholic worldview. What I am suggesting is that Catholic schools have to constantly review the coherence of the message that they are giving to their students. For many pragmatic reasons, often associated with maintaining financial viability, it is tempting for schools to overemphasise societal assumptions. They justify this by assuring themselves that the essentially Catholic disposition of the school compensates for this. But what message do the students actually receive? Is the balance between the tensions mentioned weighted in favour of a Catholic worldview? Do all headteachers believe it is legitimate to do so?

My own experience in Catholic education suggests that senior leaders do have a passionate desire to promote a Catholic vision of reality and to pass on to their students the faith that gives their own lives meaning and purpose. They often give inspiring testimony in assemblies and are among the Church's best preachers. But is this enough? What assumptions underpin decision-making in the school? What assumptions underpin the heroic efforts to achieve the best possible academic results?

What will our students have left when they have forgotten all that they learnt at school? What kind of people will they have become? Will they have a Catholic worldview? How Catholic will the curriculum that they experienced have been and to what extent will it have helped to shape their future lives?

Endnotes

1   Cf. W.R. Niblett, *Education and the Modern Mind*, (London: Faber and Faber, 1954), pp. 15 & 105.

2   J. Dewey, 'My Pedagogic Creed' in *The School Journal*, Vol LIV (3), January

16, 1897, pp. 77–80. [Also available in the *informal education archives*, https://infed.org/mobi/john-dewey-my-pedagogical-creed/. Retrieved: 29/06/2020].

3   Cf. R. Pring,'What is an educated person?' Address to Education Forum, Maynooth, 2013, https://www.maynoothuniversity.ie/sites/default/files/assets/document/Prof%20Richard%20Pring.pdf. [Retrieved: 01/07/2020].

4   M.I. Worsley, *The Development of Roman Catholic Education in Birmingham: From the Early Nineteenth Century to c 1970: Provision and Control*, Unpublished PhD Thesis, University of Birmingham, 2004, p. 78.

5   Niblett, *Education and the Modern Mind*, p. 12.

6   Cf. J. Arthur, *The Ebbing Tide: Policy & Principles of Catholic Education*, (Leominster: Gracewing, 1995).

7   Cf. B. O'Keeffe, 'Catholic Schools in an Open Society: The English Challenge' in V.A. McClelland (ed), *Aspects of Education: The Catholic School and The European Context*, (Hull: University of Hull Press, 1992), no, 46; J. O'Keefe, 'No Margin, No Mission', in McLaughlin et al. (eds) *The Contemporary Catholic School*; B. O'Keeffe, 'Reordering Perspectives in Catholic Schools' in M.P. Hornsby-Smith (ed), *Catholics in England 1950–2000: Historical and Sociological Perspectives*, (London: Cassell, 1999), p. 243.

8   Cf. Groome, 'What Makes a Catholic School?' and C.J. Richardson, 'Catholic schools and a Catholic way of seeing the world' in *The Pastoral Review*, January/February 2013, pp. 33–36, (My Modules, Module 1 Literature Resources).

CHAPTER TEN

Spiritual Development in Catholic Schools

Introduction

The importance of providing a spiritual education was enshrined in the 1944 Education Act, because 'spiritual' captured something that was generally accepted as important. What it meant was less clear, and it may have been its ambiguity that recommended it to the legislators. This ambiguity has increased over the years since the Act, as many people turn away from a spirituality based on a religious belief and embrace an inner life spirituality, searching for the authentic 'self' and personal transformation. How, then, are Catholic schools to characterise spirituality if they are to avoid simply reinforcing popular interpretations that either promote introspection and individualism or seek a vague 'lifeforce'?

What is Spirituality?

Sociologists are generally in agreement that the anticipated secularisation of the West has taken a different course than was originally predicted. Although many people have rejected organised religion, the majority still claim to be spiritual. What they mean by this is not always clear, and scholars who discuss spirituality all offer their own definition of the concept. Four recurring themes run through all these definitions. First, spirituality is fundamental to the human condition. Without it we are denied the full potential of what it means to be human. Second, spirituality is an awareness of an ultimate and enduring reality which is nonmaterial and unites us with other people and the whole of creation. Third, it is concerned with the inner life, the essence of being that shapes our individual identity and personal existence. Fourth, it animates and sustains us, giving life meaning and purpose. It is the source of inspiration and direction for life, informing our deepest values.

Known by its Effects

One of the difficulties with defining spirituality is that it is only known by its effects. It is easier to say what it does, or brings about, than what it is. The handbook for the inspections of schools directs inspectors to look for effects when evaluating spiritual development. They judge the extent to which pupils reflect on the beliefs, experiences and perspectives that shape the way that they see the world. They assess whether pupils exhibit a sense of enjoyment and fascination in learning about themselves, other people and the world around them. They look for evidence that pupils adopt imaginative and creative approaches in their learning.[1]

The broad definitions of spirituality and the anticipated effects of positive spiritual development are designed to be inclusive of people with very different understandings of spirituality. Those with a religious faith can accept all the above and so, too, can many humanists, although some consider spirituality to be meaningless.[2] There are also people, who experience what they call the 'spiritual' in their lives but are reluctant to define or conceptualise it because they feel that language cannot capture its breadth.

Breath of Life

For Catholics, the spirit is eternal and nonmaterial and flows through all of life uniting us with other people, the whole of creation and the transcendent ultimate reality and truth that we call God. It is a life-giving stream that begins as a tributary that is me, joins the river that is other people and flows into the sea that is God. In the Hebrew scripture, the word that we translate as spirit is *ruach*. There is no separate word for spirit in Hebrew. *Ruach* is spirit but also wind and breath. Wind is known by its effects and is unpredictable. Breath animates us and gives us life. It was with breath that God brought creation to life. *Ruach* is only used figuratively to mean spirit, suggesting that it has the same qualities as wind and breath.

Spirit and Matter

The spirit is distinct from the body, which is material but is not separate from it. In the early Church, there was no matter/spirit duality. In the New Testament, 'spiritual' (*pneumatikos*) is never seen as standing apart from 'bodily' (*samatikos*). The spiritual influenced the whole of life. St Paul contrasts the strength of spiritual living with the frailty of human nature. For the early Church, spiritual meant godly or generous living. During the Middle Ages, theological reflection that borrowed from classical philosophy resulted in a separation of matter and spirit, which were regarded as distinct, dichotomous entities.

This separation was evident, if not made explicit, to those of us who were educated before Vatican II. Spiritual men (priests) did spiritual things (said Mass) in spiritual places (churches) and the ordinary people were permitted to come and watch. They then went away and got on with their lives. God was remote and distant. One might say that God was somewhere else. The divine had little to do with the human other than when you received the Sacraments. Some people prayed at home and perhaps said the rosary but generally 'the spiritual' (not that we called it that at the time) was essentially for Sundays. This reinforced the separation between matter and spirit, nature and grace, the human and divine.

Vatican II retrieved the earlier understanding of nature and grace.[3] Grace, a gratuitous gift of a loving God, infuses the whole of creation. Nature is grace-filled. Through grace we can embrace this gift or reject it, but it is always present drawing us towards its source. No longer is God somewhere else. Now God is here with us. The Vatican II universal call to holiness reflects this. The epistemological origin of 'holy' is 'holistic' and all people are called to 'wholeness'. This wholeness was to be reflected in all aspects of life and bring wholeness to daily life through the participation of these spirit-filled people. No longer were the people to be observers at the Eucharist. Now they were encouraged to be conscious and active participants. Most significantly, they could no longer content themselves with Sunday spirituality. They were spiritual beings called to make the presence of God felt in the world.

Knowing Ourselves

Only a superficial life can be lived without embracing the spirit. The spiritual life is deeper, richer and more fulfilling because it allows us to become more fully human. If we are to become more fully human, we must first know ourselves at a deep level, free from pretence. We must strip away the self-delusions about who we are, based on who we would like ourselves to be, and discover the real self. We must drop our defences, face our strengths and weaknesses, embrace vulnerability. The great mystics such as Teresa of Ávila and John of the Cross found the ground of their being through inner reflection. Ignatius Loyola's spiritual exercises encourage participants to seek a clearer understanding of themselves as part of their spiritual journey.

In the television program 'The Monastery', Fr Christopher Jamison, who at the time was Abbot of Worth, invited a small group of lay people with varying levels of religious affiliation or, indeed, affinity with religion, to experience the Benedictine spiritual routine.[4] The most demanding part of this proved to be the long periods spent in silence. Most of the participants experienced dark periods as they began to peel back the façade of their lives and come to a clearer realisation of who they really were. This was a painful process and required the accompaniment of experienced spiritual advisers, found from among the monks.

Transcending Ourselves

This was not the end of the journey. The self was not a new idol for them to worship as might sometimes appear to be the case with nonreligious spiritual journeys. Indeed, overcoming a preoccupation with the self is one of the aims of the spiritual journey. This self-transcendence sensitises the individual to the urging of the Holy Spirit. However, if we have not made progress with knowing ourselves, then this may be a search conducted wearing a blindfold. For the Christian, it is this Spirit of God that animates them, and they bear witness to this in their lives. It is the knowledge that they share in the life of God and are invited to be fully united with God when they die that gives life meaning and purpose. The human spirit (lower case s), which arises from the breath of God, is 'holy'. However, it is not the Holy Spirit (upper case S), the third person of the Trinity. St Irenaeus taught that the spirit was part of a person and once united with the Holy Spirit makes a person whole.[5] The Holy Spirit leads them to fullness of life by inviting them to follow the teaching and example of Jesus. Through the Holy Spirit they come to recognise the mystery of creation.

Being Human

This descent into the depth of our being is not an attempt to escape from the realities of life but rather to be more able to embrace them. Thomas Merton was clear that our primary obligation was to be what we were created to be, namely human.[6] We don't nurture the spiritual life, we don't become holy by becoming less human. Turning our eyes to God does not involve turning our eyes away from all that is human.[7] Edward Schillebeeckx's insight that "the mystery that is man is in the deepest sense the mystery of God",[8] does not contradict the teaching of *Gaudium et Spes* that "only in the mystery of the Word made flesh does the mystery of man become clear."[9] There is not so much a paradox here as a circularity. The better we understand our humanity the better able we are to know Christ and the better we come to know Christ the more we understand ourselves.

Communal Spirituality

Whereas most nonreligious spirituality is individualistic, highlighting autonomy and self-determination, Christian spirituality is communal. Not only do we come to understand ourselves and receive God's grace through our relationship with others, but we are also able to discern whether the inner voice that we hear is from the Holy Spirit or not. If the Christian is not to be misled, if our lives are to be transformed by the Spirit so that we can develop a life-giving relationship with Christ, then we need to learn the discipline of discernment. The weakness of the human condition is such that we readily accept as the guidance of the Spirit anything that reinforces our own preferences and prejudices. The *sensus fidei*, that supernatural appreciation of the faith guaranteed by the Holy Spirit is not an assurance of personal infallibility.

It is through prayer and reflection in the light of Scripture and tradition, under the guidance of the *Magisterium* that we begin to discern where the Spirit is leading us. It is through open dialogue conducted with respect, restraint, humility and love that a clearer sense of where we are being led emerges. Nor must we assume that the oldest and wisest know best or indeed that the ordained will always be the most receptive of the Spirit's guidance. St Benedict was clear that all the brothers should be called for counsel because "the Lord often reveals what is better to the younger."[10]

Religion and Spirituality

Although one can be spiritual and not religious, the opposite is not true. Someone who is religious, who has a belief in an ultimate being towards whom they are drawn, has a particular spirituality. Catholicism is an invitation to a relationship with God. Spirituality and religion are mutually dependent for the Catholic. Religious practices reinforce our spirituality and are also an expression of that spirituality. We are seeking to become what we believe.

Active and Passive

The Catholic spiritual tradition has always encouraged a balance between active charity and passive contemplation. Three of the great architects of that tradition, St Augustine, St Gregory the Great and St Thomas Aquinas all agree that both are important.[11] Few have genuinely mystical experiences. Most people strive to develop their spiritual life through prayer and a prayerful reading of Scripture (*lectio Divina*), participation in liturgy, examination of their conscience—trying to eliminate faults and celebrating virtues and love of neighbour. For St Thérèse of Lisieux, inspired by love and trusting in God, it was performing the simplest everyday tasks well that mattered. Everyone is different, and God calls us all in different ways. John Henry Newman said that if we trust in God, he will lead us to what is best for us.[12]

Spiritual Development in Schools

Spiritual development is a lifelong process. In Catholic schools, we can only accompany our students on their journey of discovery. For some we will need to awaken the desire for this journey, which is always present within them but can be crowded out by life and contemporary culture. Teachers don't expect to see the work of spiritual development completed by the time their students leave school. What they are trying to do is to help the students realise that they are on a spiritual journey, to learn what some of the signs are along the way and how they might make progress along the road.

Teachers need to help their pupils to see beyond the apparent and to reflect on their experiences so that they can begin to discern the presence of God in themselves and the whole of creation. This can begin by taking delight in being human and celebrating all that they are able to do. Teachers with an infectious enthusiasm for their subjects can help them to appreciate the mystery present in every subject discipline, whether it is everything new to the youngest pupils or the margins of knowledge for the eldest.

What is often called 'emotional intelligence' is important for spiritual development. Pupils need to begin to understand themselves and their relationship with others. Here, creative and expressive arts can play an important part and should not be regarded as peripheral subjects. Here also there is a need to experience silence and stillness: a time for reflection and prayer. In the noisy, stimulating and constantly moving world in which they live, time must be created when they can experience the tranquillity of silence and the balm of inactivity.

The way that the school is organised and the values that underpin its operation should reflect the unity of spirit and matter. The spiritual should permeate everything within the school and not be relegated to special events and occasions such as assembly and RE lessons. Liturgy should not be an occasional feature of school life but regular, planned and thoroughly prepared. The role of the chaplain should be incorporated into the life of the school, and care should be taken that other staff do not leave 'religious' or 'spiritual' things to him or her.

Nurturing the Nurturers

Spiritual development is about accompaniment. But those who walk alongside others must have developed their own spiritual life because, after all, you can't share what you don't have. As Cardinal Hume pointed out, this does not imply that teachers have found all the answers to the spiritual meaning of their lives but that they are genuinely searching for those answers themselves.[13] Teachers must find time in their own busy lives to seek these answers and recharge their spiritual batteries. Making this a priority is not easy. There are no Ofsted boxes to tick regarding your own spiritual life. When something has to give, it is easy for periods of inactivity to be sacrificed in order to complete some marking, plan a lesson or phone a worried parent.

Endnotes

1   Ofsted, *Handbook for the Inspection of Schools*, (www.gov.uk/ofsted, 2016), n. 136. [Withdrawn].

2   M. Mason, *"Spirituality"—What on Earth Is It?* Paper given at the International Conference of Children's Spirituality at Roehampton Institute, Summer 2000.

3   Cf. J. Hanvey & A. Carroll, *On the Way of Life*, (London: CES, 2006), pp. 39–41.

4   Cf. C. Jamison, *Finding Sanctuary: monastic steps for everyday life*, (London: Weidenfeld & Nicolson, 2006).

5   Irenaeus, 'Against Heresies' V.vi.1, in A. Roberts & J. Donaldson (eds.), *The Ante-Nicene Fathers. I. The Apostolic Fathers with Justin Martyr and Irenaeus* (Grand Rapids, MI: Eerdmans, 1993), p. 531.

6   Cf. T. Merton, *Contemplation in a World of Action*, (South Bend, IN: University of Notre Dame Press, 1998), p. 83. Quoted in D. Carrera, 'Standing before God: Merton's Incarnational Spirituality' *TMA* 16, 2003, pp. 56–72.

7   Cf. T. Merton, *New Seeds of Contemplation*, (New York: New Direction Books, 1961), p. 39. Quoted in Carrera, 'Standing before God: Merton's Incarnational Spirituality'.

8   E. Schillebeeckx, *The Mission of the Church*, (London: Sheed & Ward, 1973), p. 79.

9   *GS*, n. 22.

10   Benedict of Nusia, *St Benedict's Rule for Monasteries*, Translated by Leonard J. Doyle, (Minnesota: The Liturgical Press, 1950).

11   Cf. J. Aumann, *Christian Spirituality in the Catholic Tradition*, (London, Sheed & Ward, 1985).

12   Cf. J.H. Newman, *Meditations and Devotions*, ed. H. Tristram, (London: Longmans Edition, 1953).

13   B. Hume, 'The Nature of Spiritual and Moral Development', in *Partners in Mission*, (London: CES, 1997), pp. 83–93.

CHAPTER ELEVEN

Dialogue: More Than a Friendly Chat

A New Orientation

Orientating the Church towards dialogue was one of the major achievements of Vatican II.[1] It marked a radical departure from what had gone immediately before. Even fifty years earlier, advocating dialogue within the Church, let alone with those outside it, would have been considered ridiculous. The prevailing view was that the Church possessed 'the truth' and had a duty to make that truth known, shining the light of truth on those with whom it came into contact. What could the Church learn from those who did not possess the truth? Error had nothing to teach believers and, indeed, was a source of danger for them. This is well illustrated, for example, in the Church's attitude to the ecumenical movement. After World War I, Catholics were forbidden from involvement in the developing ecumenical movement. As late as 1948, Pope Pius XI regarded the Mother Church's ecumenical objective as recalling her erring sons (sic) and leading them back to her bosom.[2]

Not only did dialogue insinuate itself into the language of Vatican II but during the Council, Pope Paul VI published his encyclical *Ecclesiam Suam*, which was an extended treatment of the importance of dialogue for the Church and for its relationship with other people. He recognised that dialogue was 'demanded' because the sacred and the profane were no longer seen as distinct, and the Church had to engage with the world around it. This world was made up of many different peoples with a wide variety of beliefs and ways of seeing the world. It was also a world that comprised people who could no longer be treated like children.[3]

Catholic Schools, Places of Dialogue

Dialogue also found its way into the Declaration on Catholic Education, *Gravissimum Educationis*. The template for this declaration, *Divini Illius Magister*, issued by Pope Pius XI in 1929, did not mention dialogue. The Vatican II declaration mentions it twice, as does the first document produced by the Congregation for Catholic Education (CCE) in 1977. The Congregation's 1982 document mentions it eleven times. It is a regular feature of subsequent documents including the one in 2013 dedicated to intercultural dialogue.

Catholic schools are places of dialogue, where the Gospel is given a privileged hearing. For many young people, school is the only place where they will come into contact with the Gospel. The preliminary document for the World Congress on Catholic Education held in 2015 acknowledges the value of dialogue in bringing young people to an understanding of "truth, good and beauty." It recognises that communication between students and teachers is circular rather than unidirectional, and also that there is a need for teachers to provide "credible testimony" rather than relying on the weight of their authority.[4]

Talking Together

What, then, is this 'dialogue' with which we are encouraged to engage? The word itself is derived from two Greek words *dia*, meaning across or together and *logos*, which means words or talking. Dialogue can be taken to mean talking together. It is, however, much more than a casual conversation and is certainly to be distinguished from alternating monologues where people speak in turn without really hearing what the other has to say. The ground-breaking insights into the meaning of dialogue were provided by the existentialist philosopher Martin Buber[5] in the early twentieth century, and his influence can be felt in ecclesial documents from Vatican II onwards.[6]

Understanding the Other and Ourselves

For Buber, dialogue is not just an attempt to understand another person's argument or point of view but an attempt to understand the other person taken as a whole. It recognises the other person as an equal and not as someone to whom something must be done; not simply someone for us to convince. This *I/Thou* relationship, as he described it, regards both participants as subjects and neither as objects. According to Buber, it is through such a dialogical relationship that we come to understand ourselves as well as the other person. He saw God as the eternal *Thou*, and the relationship between individuals and God as the foundation of all other relationships.

Dialogue is a process aimed at mutual understanding. A journey along a road without a predetermined destination. A journey which enriches both parties. Among its prerequisites are trust, open-mindedness and a willingness to listen. It requires the courage to open oneself up to another and risk having to change one's opinion. It requires the humility to accept that truth is beyond the grasp of an individual, and to respect the worth of an alternative point of view. The values that underpin dialogue and give it integrity and vitality cannot simply be adopted for the occasion. They have to be intrinsic to participants, values that inform their life. This is why Buber sees dialogue as an authentic way of being.

Types of Dialogue

Dialogue can take a number of forms. Plato argued that thought was a form of internal dialogue. When we grapple with a new idea and weigh it against what we already know, we engage in a form of dialogue between conflicting perspectives with the aim of arriving at a new or enhanced level of understanding. This is a good metaphor for dialogue with another person where we are not dismissive of an alternative point of view but rather consider it an opportunity to gain new insights.

It is often argued that dialogue is a rational activity because without the underlying logical structure of the discussion it would be impossible to proceed. This is no doubt correct, but dialogue also requires a degree of empathy, of understanding feelings. In our current age, emotions and experience often inform the language with which we express our opinions.

Dialogue is not just about talking. It can involve sharing the "joys and the hopes, the griefs and the anxieties"[7] of everyday life. Behaviour is another form of dialogue. How we act is an expression of who we are and what we stand for. In a sense life is dialogical. Our contact with other people changes us and them.

Barriers to Dialogue

There are barriers to dialogue, some more significant than others. Any attempts to deceive, coerce or exploit negates dialogue. Insults, ridicule and even rhetoric are proscribed. Dialogue tries to get beyond prejudice, disputes about the meaning of words, generalisations and ideology as it seeks understanding. Even tolerance can be a barrier because it respects the integrity of the status quo whilst dialogue does not regard any position as static but rather as organic. Dialogue seeks mutual transformation.

Another barrier is our Western adherence to the law of noncontradiction, that something cannot be true and false at the same time. Other philosophical traditions are not constrained by this. The Catholic Church often claims to embrace 'and/as well' rather than 'either/or'. We profess that God is three and God is one. We acknowledge Christ as fully God and fully man. Paradox can be instructive. The end of the prayer of St Francis acknowledges that "in giving we receive, in forgiving we are forgiven and in dying we are born to eternal life." Noncontradiction can be a barrier to dialogue, which often requires apparently contradictory positions to be set alongside each other.

It can be argued that doctrine is a barrier to dialogue. Defence of something considered immutable is incompatible with genuine dialogue. However, the Church teaches that we should engage in doctrinal dialogue with courage and accept that this may result in a need to revise our own position.[8] Pope Benedict XVI, writing as Joseph Ratzinger, argued that mission and dialogue should not be seen as opposites but rather should "mutually interpenetrate". According to Pope Benedict, allowing my own limited understanding of truth to be broken down helps me to gain a better understanding of the truth about God, which I can never fully comprehend.[9] Doctrine and dialogue can be seen as different aspects of an evangelical process as long as they are approached with intellectual humility.[10]

There are those who have reservations about dialogue and worry that it erodes the authority of the bishops, obscures Church teaching and elevates the status of dissent. They remind us that dialogue is not the only form of communication in the Church and that proclamation plays an important part. Others invoke the *sensus fidei* and argue that where Scripture and tradition inform the dialogue, then faith and practice are enriched. Perhaps this is fertile ground for genuine dialogue.[11]

Harmonious Tension

Schools are dialogical institutions providing a venue for contrasting validity claims to dialogue with each other. As a Catholic community, where we acknowledge the presence of God among us, we strive for dialogue, which allows different points of view to be held in harmonious tension. As on many other occasions when we discuss our faith, we are drawn back to the Trinity. Here we find harmonious tension. Here we find the theological underpinning of our commitment to dialogue.

Dialogue Between Faith and Culture

The documents emanating from the Congregation for Catholic Education speak frequently of the importance of schools in providing opportunities for dialogue between faith and culture in the hope that this will eventually lead to a synthesis of these. Indeed, the Church teaches that "man comes to a true and full humanity only through culture."[12] In part, this synthesis is modelled in the lives of Catholics on the staff who demonstrate how to live an authentic Christian life within the culture that they inhabit. In a sense, they are the answer to the question, 'how can I be a Christian in the modern world'. That they sometimes fail to live up to what they profess is part of the example that they give. The weaknesses of the human condition often cause us to fail but once we acknowledge our shortcomings, we can pick ourselves up and try again.

The dialogue between faith and culture also involves trying to understand what it is that we believe and what we can learn from culture. The Church has a history of being dismissive of dominant cultural trends. During the late nineteenth and early twentieth century 'modernism' was condemned and with it new ways of studying Scripture. During the twentieth century popes have condemned many 'isms' of the 'postmodern' world such as relativism, individualism and syncretism. Rarely are the positive elements of modern culture celebrated. Is enough attention given to the rise of ecology, feminism and spirituality?[13] Is enough attention paid to what our students actually think?[14] If we are to walk with them on their journey of faith and help them to understand the relevance of the Gospel for their lives, then we must first listen to them as Jesus did to the disciples on the road to Emmaus.

Respect Different Perspectives

Catholic schools are also engaged in dialogue with Christians of other denominations, people of other faiths and nonbelievers. Respect for these differing perspectives is a prerequisite for dialogue. Helping people to walk along the path that they are on and reflecting an understanding of the meaning it holds for them, builds trust and helps them to see how the light of the Gospel can bring their own path into sharper relief. In particular, appreciation must be shown for those "who are honestly seeking God according to his or her own conscience".[15] Nor should we ignore those who claim to have no belief in God. Often, they have a sense of being part of something greater than themselves, and this provides common ground for exploration.

I remember talking with three head students, sixth formers, at a Salesian school. We discussed their experience of being in the school. One was a Catholic, one an Anglican and the third a Hindu. It was evident from what they told me that they had been strongly influenced by the school's ethos. They reflected on their experience of a school where Christian values permeated daily life. Respect for others was promoted and individual difference valued. Genuine dialogue had taken place between students, with staff and between the assumptions that individuals brought from home and the values that the school promoted and modelled. Their reflections were shaped by the distinctive educational charism of Don Bosco. I was left with the impression that although they would not all become Catholics, that they would always be Salesians.

In the Light of The Gospel

Critically, dialogue takes place in RE lessons. Well-managed lessons led by knowledgeable and enthusiastic teachers create an ideal environment for genuine dialogue. Here, students can express their opinions and explore alternative points of view, but the Gospel is always given a respectful hearing. If the Gospel is not clearly presented and explained, and if students are not able to explore their own views in the light of the Gospel, then an important opportunity for dialogue is lost.

I have visited many good Catholic schools over the years, but one secondary school that I inspected illustrates the significant role of dialogue in RE lessons. The students, including the fifteen- and sixteen-year-olds, spoke enthusiastically about their RE lessons. They enjoyed the open discussions that took place. On observing lessons, it was clear that genuine dialogue was taking place. The teacher had created an environment where people were confident to express their opinions whilst listening respectfully to the opinions of others. One particular discussion was about the Church's teaching on birth control. The teacher explained Catholic teaching clearly and a wide-ranging, insightful dialogue ensued. The students did not all leave the room accepting the Church's teaching, but they did leave having a better understanding of the issue and what the Church taught and why. It was clear from other conversations with these students that they had an enormous respect for the teacher and felt that they were constantly challenged to revise their preconceptions about many issues.

Conclusion

Catholic schools provide an arena where constructive dialogue can take place. However, this should not be left to chance. Schools must be mindful of the contexts within which dialogue occurs, nurture the attitudes required for genuine dialogue and ensure that members of staff have the necessary understanding of the faith to give a coherent account of it in word and deed.

Endnotes

1 Cf. J.W. O'Malley, *What Happened at Vatican II*, (Cambridge Mass.: Harvard University Press, 2008).

2 Pope Pius XI, *Mortalium Animos* (Vatican website, 1928), n.4.

3   Cf. Pope Paul VI, *Ecclesiam Suam* (Vatican website, 1964), n.78.

4   CCE, *Educating Today and Tomorrow: A renewing passion, Instrumentum laboris*, (www.educatio.va, 2015, pp. 11/12).

5   M. Buber, *I and Thou* (2nd Ed.), Translated by Ronald Gregor Smith, (New York: Scribner's Sons, 1958).

6   Cf. Benedict XVI, *Speech to the General Assembly of the Italian Bishops' Conference* (www.vatican.va, 27 May 2010).

7   *GS*, n.1.

8   Cf. Secretariat for Unbelievers, 'Humanae Personae Dignitatem' in A. Flannery, *Vatican Council II* (Leominster: Fowler Wright 1981), p.1007.

9   J. Ratzinger, *Many Religions and One Covenant*, (San Francisco: Ignatius Press, 1998), pp.110–112 & 202.

10 S. Caldecott, 'Benedict XVI and Inter-Religious Dialogue' in *Transformation*, 23/4 October 2006.

11 Cf. B. Hinze, *Practices of Dialogue in the Roman Catholic Church* (New York: Continuum, 2006), pp.114–118.

12 *GS*, n. 53.

13 P.M. Gallagher, *Clashing Symbols: An Introduction to Faith & Culture*, (London: Darton, Longman & Todd, 1997), p. 110.

14 Cf. S. Savage, S. Collins-Mayo, B. Mayo & G. Cray, *Making sense of Generation Y: The World View of 15- to 25-year-olds*, (London: Church House Publishing, 2006).

15 CCE, *Lay Catholics in Schools*, n. 42.

CHAPTER TWELVE

Eucharist: Sacrificial Memorial and Sacred Banquet

Introduction

As a lifelong Catholic, the Eucharist is not only a central feature of my religious practice but an enduring and mysterious reservoir of grace from which I am sent out to sanctify the world, something that I no doubt do inadequately. This balance, which St Augustine saw as between contemplation and recognising our neighbour's needs,[1] can be distorted by an inward-looking, Eucharist-focused spirituality that fails to recognise either the incarnational spirituality associated with making Christ present in the world, or the Church's declared preferential option for the poor and marginalised.

Almost as soon as the Vatican II liturgical reforms had begun, concerns began to be expressed regarding 'abuses'.[2] Some of the concerns were no doubt raised by those who objected to the reforms or failed to understand their significance. However, the *Magisterium* began to be concerned that an overemphasis on the Mass as a banquet, interpreted by some as a fraternal meal, was obscuring the central sacrificial focus of the eucharistic liturgy. To redress the balance, several documents were produced that stressed the importance of the sacrificial nature of the Mass.

Two of the most significant documents were the Encyclical *Ecclesia De Eucharistia* and the post synodal Apostolic Exhortation *Sacramentum*

Caritatis (*SCar*). Whilst following *Sacrosanctum Concilium* (*SC*) in stressing that it was a eucharistic sacrifice that the Lord instituted,[3] these documents also acknowledge that it is a "paschal banquet",[4] food for a journey[5] which makes the faithful feel more obliged to fulfil their duties as citizens[6] and allows the great mystery to be lived[7] and to be carried over into our daily lives.[8] However, as the primary purpose of the documents was to reaffirm the central sacrificial focus of the Mass, these other aspects were relegated to the end of the document and are not always given the prominence that they deserve when pastors are encouraging their people to develop a greater reverence for the Eucharist.

Altar and Table

In *Ecclesia De Eucharistia* Pope St John Paul II uses the description "altar" and "table of the Lord" interchangeably. Altar is a more cultic term denoting a place where sacrifice is offered. Table is more commonly associated with a family meal. It is unsurprising that Pope St John Paul II uses both terms, as the altar of sacrifice and the table of the Lord are, after all, aspects of the same mystery.[9] He is quite clear that it is always a sacrificial banquet that we celebrate,[10] but his juxtaposition of the two terms indicates that he is trying to keep an appropriate balance between different elements of a complex whole.

Striking a Balance

As in all things pertaining to the faith, we need to ensure that we strike the correct balance between different elements. A singular emphasis on sacrifice may lead people to believe that worship can be detached from love of neighbour. A singular emphasis on banquet may lead people to believe that love of neighbour can be detached from worship. As we know, the two are intimately linked. Loving God with heart, soul and strength may be the first commandment but loving our neighbour just as intensely is not an optional extra (Lk 10:27). It is no surprise that although we are encouraged to follow the Lord's instruction and pray alone in the privacy of our own room (Matt 6:6), the most important liturgical celebration is communal.

Source and Summit

The Church's teaching on the Eucharist is rich and goes right to the heart of what it means to be a Catholic. *Lumen Gentium* states unequivocally that the eucharistic sacrifice is "the source and summit of the Christian life."[11] It is here that we come into direct contact with the risen Christ, who is both the centre of our Christian life and our ultimate destiny. Through the Eucharist, Christ sustains us for life's journey and prepares us for union with him in heaven. Pope St John Paul II called the Eucharist "a priceless treasure" because through it we "make contact with the very wellspring of grace."[12]

At the Eucharist, we are invited to participate in the institution of the sacrament, the drama of Christ's passion and death, and the glory of his resurrection. It is the constant teaching of the Church that it is the sacrificial element of the Eucharist that gives it potency. On Calvary, Christ offered himself to the Father for our salvation. During the Eucharist, Christ continues to offer himself to the Father through the priest, who acts in *persona Christi*. This is not another sacrifice but the same sacrifice as was offered on Calvary. We are caught up in this paschal mystery, where the whole Church offers itself to the Father.[13] Through this, we become both the celebrant and the sacrifice as we offer ourselves with Christ through the action of the priest.[14] The priest not only acts in *persona Christi* but also represents all of us, acting *in persona ecclesiae*.

It is Wonderful to Be Here

Like the Israelites at the exodus from Egypt, who passed over from slavery to freedom, we pass over from sin and death to everlasting life. We confront the mystery of faith and proclaim that by Christ's cross and resurrection he has set us free, that he is the saviour of the world. We could easily find ourselves repeating the words of St Peter at the transfiguration, "It is wonderful for us to be here" (Matt 17:4). No wonder this is regarded as a mystery of faith. Pope Paul VI recognised how daunting this teaching was and advised us to approach the mystery "with humility and reverence" and not to rely on human reason but rather on what God has revealed to us.[15]

For Catholics, the centrality of the Eucharist is a given. It is not only a source of grace but also a profound act of faith. To recognise God in bread and wine and to bow down in veneration challenges the nonbeliever, who may find it incomprehensible. This act of faith is taken further during exposition of the Blessed Sacrament, when the faithful spend time in silent prayer and contemplation in the presence of the risen Lord. Given that Christ is really, 'substantially' present in the Eucharist, it is unsurprising that the faithful want to spend time in his presence. It is the closest that we can come to the risen Christ in this life and, consequently, is not only the source of grace but the summit of our spiritual life. All that we do stems from our faith in Christ's presence and all that we do is drawn back to his presence.

Eschatological Purpose

However, *Sacrosanctum Concilium* is quite clear that the "sacred liturgy does not exhaust the entire activity of the Church."[16] There is no suggestion in Scripture that we are created to spend our entire lives kneeling before the Blessed Sacrament. The Eucharist may be the source and summit of the Christian life, but it is not its purpose. The Lord taught us that if we eat his flesh and drink his blood, we will have eternal life and be raised up on the last day (Jn 6:54). It is this eternal life, where we will know him as he really is (1 Jn 3:2) that is our ultimate eschatological purpose (the final end to which we are travelling). The Eucharist is a foretaste of that heavenly state and through it "God joins himself to us in the most perfect union."[17] But this close relationship with God can be lost through sin. Indeed, we can only have a communion with God that is alive and true if we live communion among ourselves.[18] Our ultimate purpose is that permanent relationship with God that the righteous are promised after their earthly life is complete.

Doing the Will of The Father

The Lord commended Mary for sitting at his feet and listening to his words rather than helping Martha with her many chores (Lk 10:38-42). However, this is essentially a reminder that heeding the word of Jesus is the most important thing for us to do.[19] It is also an instruction about the importance of renewal and recognising our need for God's help in all things. But we are told quite firmly that it is not those who cry, "'Lord, Lord' who will enter the Kingdom of heaven but those who do the will of my Father" (Matt 7:21), and the will of the Father is that we should love one another (Jn 13:34). It is in loving one another that we fulfil God's plan for us. God made us as a supreme act of love and to fulfil his own purpose. In cooperating with this divine plan, we do the good works that have been allocated to us (cf. Eph 2:10). As the catechism says, in fulfilling his purpose "God grants his creatures not only their existence, but also the dignity of acting on their own...of cooperating in the accomplishment of his plan."[20] If we have the courage and fortitude to use the gifts and talents that we have received from God, then we can help to build a society powered by love, and it is the Eucharist, "the food of truth [that] gives us renewed strength and courage to work tirelessly in the service of the civilisation of love."[21]

Food for A Journey

When the Lord instituted the Eucharist, he did not say 'this is my body, worship it'. Rather he said, 'this is my body, eat it'. The Council of Trent made it clear that the Blessed Sacrament should be venerated and adored despite being instituted to be received.[22] Pope Benedict XVI says that distinguishing between worshipping and receiving is a false dichotomy because anyone who acknowledges Christ's presence in the Eucharist will want to worship it.[23] He quotes St Augustine, who argues that it would be sinful not to worship before we consume. Catholics accept this, and it has long been a familiar feature of popular piety. However, this does not seem to have been in Jesus' mind at the institution of the Eucharist. He was not giving us an object for worship but food to sustain us on a journey. He emphasises that the bread and wine have become his body and blood, which has been broken and poured out for us—indicating its sacrificial significance. He instructs us to take it and eat it and to do all this as a commemoration of him. The Eucharist is food for a journey and that journey takes us out into the world to "work for the sanctification of the world from within."[24]

A growing emphasis on the Eucharist as a fraternal banquet resulted in a corrective re-emphasis on the sacrificial nature of the Paschal mystery. But the Eucharist is both sacrifice and banquet, "a true banquet, in which Christ offers himself as our nourishment."[25] Surely maintaining the balance here is important lest we forget our mission to the world at large and mislead ourselves into believing that if we celebrate the Eucharist, we are doing all that is required of us when, in fact, it is only by doing other things correctly that we are disposed to receive the Blessed Sacrament worthily (1 Cor 11:17–22, 27–34).

Sent Out

The Gospel is full of exhortations to reach out to those in need. Not only must we eat the flesh of the Son of Man if we are to have eternal life, but we must also recognise Christ in the poor and marginalised (Matt 35:21–46). If we confine ourselves to the safety of our churches and enjoy the fruits of Christ's sacrifice without recognising Lazarus at our gates, then we are likely to be condemned (Lk 16:19–31). In receiving the Eucharist, we are more closely conformed to Christ. In fact, we become what we have received.[26] This makes us more sensitive to the suffering of others and committed to finding ways to alleviate them.[27] It strengthens us to exercise our mission to the world, which is to "seek the Kingdom of God by engaging in temporal affairs and ordering them according to the plan of God."[28] As *Lumen Gentium* tells us, if we are to achieve perfection, we must conform ourselves to Christ and do the will of the Father. We must devote ourselves to the glory of God and the service of our neighbours.[29]

The celebration of the Eucharist does not end with the sacrifice. We are not sent out from the Mass in despair. Rather, we are filled with hope in the resurrection. Our hope and joy is one of the ways in which the face of Christ shines forth from the Church providing light for the nations.[30] We go out to live what we have proclaimed (1 Cor 11:26) and to fulfil God's will in our daily lives.[31] As the catechism says so powerfully, "To receive in truth the Body and Blood of Christ given up for us, we must recognise Christ in the poorest, his brethren."[32]

Conclusion

The Eucharist is not an end in itself but a crucial means to a more complete end. Importantly, the Eucharist is a commemoration of Christ's sacrifice, but it is also a paschal banquet, food for a journey, and this is not a journey that we take alone. It is a journey that we share with our fellow travellers. It is no doubt right and fitting that pastors should encourage a profound respect for the Eucharist and remind the faithful of its central significance in the economy of salvation. Surely, however, they should also help them to understand that the Eucharist does not close them in on themselves but opens them up to other people. It should encourage us to bear witness to our faith[33] and work for a more just and fraternal society.[34] It is a gratuitous gift from a loving God and one that we give thanks for, not only through the liturgy but also through our lives.

Endnotes

1. Augustine, *City of God*, Book XIX, chapter 19.
2. Cf. Sacred Congregation for the Sacraments and Divine Worship, Instruction Concerning Worship of The Eucharistic Mystery, *Inaestimabile Donum* (Vatican City, 1980).
3. Cf. *SC*, n. 47.
4. Cf. ibid., *EE*, n. 16.
5. *EE*, n. 62.
6. ibid., n. 20.
7. *SCar*, n. 79.
8. ibid., n. 82.
9. *CCC*, n. 1383
10. *EE*, n. 48.
11. *LG*, n.11.
12. *EE*, n. 25.
13. Cf. Sacred Congregation for the Doctrine of the Faith, Declaration, *Inter Insigniores* (Vatican website, 1973), n. 33.
14. Cf. *LG*, n. 10.
15. Pope Paul VI, *Mysterium Fidei* (Vatican website, 1065), n. 4.
16. *SC*, n. 9.
17. *EE*, n. 34.
18. *SCar*, n. 76.
19. R.E. Brown, *An Introduction to the New Testament*, (London: Yale University Press, 2010), p. 245.
20. *CCC*, n. 306.
21. *SCar*, n. 90.
22. J. Waterworth, (ed. and trans.), *The canons and decrees of the sacred and oecumenical Council of Trent*, (London: Dolman, 1848), p. 79, Ch. V.
23. Cf. *SCar*, n. 66.
24. *LG*, n. 31.
25. *EE*, n. 16.
26. Cf. ibid., n. 36.

27 Pope St John Paul II, *Dominicae Cenae* (Vatican website, 1980), n. 6.
28 *LG*, n. 31.
29 ibid., n. 40:2.
30 ibid., n.1.
31 Cf. CCC, n. 1332.
32 ibid., n.1397.
33 Cf. Pope St John Paul II, *Mane Nobiscum Domine* (Vatican website, 2004), n. 24.
34 Cf. ibid., n 28.

CHAPTER THIRTEEN

Evangelisation: Looking for Mission-Effectiveness

A Call to Renewal

Bishop Richard Moth has asked the diocese of Arundel and Brighton to give careful consideration to the renewal that is required for 'mission-effectiveness'. Many helpful suggestions will emerge from discussion across the diocese. What I want to suggest here is that we look more deeply at the barriers to mission, which I read as synonymous with evangelisation, and avoid simply implementing suggestions that are unchallenging.

Apart from Vatican II documents there are two other major post synodal apostolic exhortations that explore and explain evangelisation. Paul VI issued *Evangelii Nuntiandi* (Sharing the Gospel) in 1975 and Francis issues *Evangelii Gaudium* (the Joy of the Gospel) in 2013. In these two documents, we find broadly similar analysis although the later document is more radical in its language. *Evangelii Nuntiandi* sees three distinct areas for evangelisation. The first is personal renewal by all the people of God. The second is a renewal of the Church itself, because it is always in need of being purified.[1] Thirdly there is a need for an in-depth conversion of our culture because we are profoundly linked to it.[2] We tend to interpret our faith within the context of our culture. If it is hostile to religious belief, then that represents a significant challenge.

Personal Renewal

Pope Francis tells us that If we are to evangelise we must start by "renewing our personal encounter with Jesus Christ."[3] Even those of us who have spent our entire lives in contact with the Gospel need to "deepen, consolidate and nourish" our faith, and allow it to mature.[4] What is called for is a re-evaluation of our values, interests and thinking, in fact everything that informs how we see the world and act in the world.[5] At its most basic, we need to form habits of prayer, worship, study and service. We need to make better use of Scripture in our daily lives perhaps learning to use *Lectio Divina* as a means of opening our hearts to God's call to us.

Evangelisation requires witnesses. Those who live the Christian life and exhibit in their words and deeds what they claim to profess. Indeed, it was the witness of the early Christians that attracted the attention of the pagans. The Gospel is proclaimed by witnesses, but these witnesses must be people of integrity, believing what they proclaim and living what they believe.[6] They must be people who find joy in the Gospel[7] and allow the face of Christ to shine forth from the Church through them.[8] They must avoid giving the impression that faith is a burden, living lives "that seem like Lent without Easter."[9]

Witnessing is only the beginning. Eventually some explanation must be given for the way we live our lives.[10] Seek the Kingdom, build it up, live it and proclaim it says Pope Paul.[11] We are not all called to be preachers or teachers, but we need to be able to offer some reasons for the hope that is within us (1 Pet 3:15). Here, we come to a critical component of any programme of evangelisation: a review of adult formation in the Church so that people can explore the best way to answer those who express an interest in the Christian way of life. Consideration also needs to be given to ways of answering critics, because a factor that discourages committed Christians from declaring their allegiance to Jesus Christ is a fear that they will be criticised and unable to refute their critics. For example, what are they to say to those who claim religious belief is delusional? How are they to answer those who find the presence of evil a barrier to belief?

Our process of personal renewal should also include discernment of the charisms, or gifts of the Spirit, that each of us has received. St Paul was clear that the early community in Corinth was blessed with a plethora of charisms

(1 Cor 12:4–11). We all have gifts and talents that we can use for the good of the community. Our gifts may be largely practical. They may be pastoral or academic. They may be identifiably relevant within a religious community, but they may be gifts that we mainly exercise out in the world.[12] They may not seem exceptional but "each believer has a right and duty to use them in the Church and the world for the good of humankind and for the upbuilding of the Church."[13] Discerning these gifts is an important stage in engaging with evangelisation.

It is important to remember that this is only a preliminary stage. We are not retreating into a holy huddle, confident in our righteousness. Pope Francis expresses forcefully what we should be doing. We must be a Church that goes forth to sow the good seed,[14] getting involved in people's lives, bridging distances between people, abasing ourselves if necessary, embracing human life and touching the flesh of Christ in others.[15] We must take on the "smell of the sheep"[16] and risk being "bruised and hurting".[17] This may be an alarming prospect, but we are not working alone. Not only is the Word of God powerful when clearly proclaimed but the Holy Spirit is at work quietly in everyone that we encounter. The soil is being prepared for the seed.

In particular, solidarity with "those who society discards"[18] is the test of authenticity for a Christian. This solidarity is not optional. Nor is it a one-way process. Pope Francis tells us that we must listen to what those we encounter on the margins of society teach us.[19] Through them we are re-evangelised.

Church Renewal

Two events were organised by the Bishops' Conference of England and Wales as part of a programme of renewal both for individuals and the Church in general. Following on from the last quadrennial International Eucharistic Congress, held in 2016 in the Philippines, the Church in England and Wales held a National Eucharistic Pilgrimage and Congress in Liverpool in June 2018. The purpose of this gathering was to strengthen the faithful in their commitment to the Real Presence of Christ in the Eucharist. This was a major exercise in nurturing evangelisation. It was also a large public display of the health of the Catholic Church, as it is estimated that 10,000 people attended.

Another major event was the triannual World Meeting of Families, which took place in Dublin in August 2018. This provided an opportunity to celebrate, pray and reflect on the importance of marriage and the family as the cornerstone of our lives. This can also be seen as an event preparing for evangelisation because the family is a critical source of evangelisation.[20]

These events have the potential to be a source of renewed fervour among those who attend. The challenge is to ensure that the benefits cascade down into parishes in a way envisaged by Bishop Richard in his pastoral message for the first Sunday of Advent when he says that the people returning to their parishes from the Eucharistic Congress 'will enable us all to renew Mission, entered on and going forth from, the Eucharist'. This will require detailed preparation and follow up at diocesan level if it is to bear fruit.

These two initiatives were excellent in themselves and had the potential to enrich the life of the Catholic community across the country. However, although there is much that is praiseworthy about the Catholic Church, there is also much that erodes our credibility in the eyes of the faithful themselves and others who we try to evangelise. Failure to recognise the deficiencies and endeavour to resolve them will seriously inhibit any attempts at evangelisation. It is beyond the scope of this paper to explore the strengths and weaknesses of the Church, but some key issues need to be addressed.

One issue is how to manage the theological pluralism that exists within the Church. What kind of Church are we inviting people to join? Is it one based on unchanging abstract propositions worked out by clever people and handed down to the faithful, or is it a Church where the truths of the faith are discerned from the lived experience of people in the light of Scripture and tradition? An incommensurability between these two approaches was evident at the 2015 Synod on the Family. If they are both legitimate aspects of the Catholic tradition, how are they to be reconciled?

What are we to do about the apparent licence of clergy to follow their own theological disposition? Some priests arrive in a parish and sweep aside years of dedicated work by former incumbents and their people. Examples abound of the re-emergence of clericalism (clergy controlled), juridicism (rule bound) and triumphalism (self-satisfied superiority) that have been disavowed by Vatican II Fathers and subsequent magisterial teaching. Unless a solution to these kinds of situations can be found, we will see more of the faithful (faithful to Christ but disillusioned with the Church) walk away, rather than an influx of new blood.

How are we going to tackle what many young people regard as hypocrisy in the Church? They cite the mishandling of the abuse cases, where it appears that there was more concern for the shepherds and the sheepfold than the sheep. They are unimpressed with the attitude of the Church to women, the failure of the Church to commit itself unreservedly to the pursuit of social justice and its obsession with sexuality. There may be a naivety behind some of these criticisms, but they would be echoed, if slightly modified, by many of the adult faithful.

The complexity and intractability of some of these issues suggests that they will not be resolved by tried and tested methods. There needs to be courage to try what is genuinely new and not just to dress up old ideas in new clothes. There is a need for a sharing of knowledge and skills right across the Church and a commitment to genuine collaboration and dialogue. This will throw up ideas that challenge existing norms, but it is necessary to embrace them. We must work with emerging solutions rather than suppress them. The Fathers of Vatican II pointed to some ways of tackling these issues. They advocated collaboration between the bishops of the world. The Fathers also pointed to the supernatural interpretation of the faith, the *sensus fidei*, which resided in all the people of God. This was not a call for democracy or to embrace communitarianism but recognition that the experience of the faithful had a valuable part to play in the life of the Church.

All this highlights the need for a formal process of discernment. During the Synod on the Family Pope Francis promoted 'synodality', inclusive of laity and ordained, saying that it was the way forward that God wants for His Church. Synodality could be national along the lines of the Pastoral Congress held in 1980. Alternatively, it could take the form of diocesan synods. Either could energise the faithful and allow the Holy Spirit to speak through the entire people of God nationally or locally. Such processes have risks of course. They might leave us bruised and hurting. But unless we tackle the critical issues facing the Church any evangelisation will be seriously impeded.

Cultural Renewal

It is difficult to judge the temperature of our culture when it comes to religion. Increasing numbers of people identify themselves as not belonging to any religious grouping. At the same time, commentators report a deep sense of disorientation among many people who do not feel comfortable within the society that they now experience. Some of this was made evident politically with the vote for Brexit and the election of Donald Trump.

What does seem clear is that there are cultural assumptions that conflict with the Gospel. This is not new. They laughed at St Paul in Athens (Acts 17:32). But unless we examine the cultural barriers to accepting the Gospel, we will even struggle to evangelise the young people who are in our schools.

There is a significant difference between the Catholic anthropology that regards us as created by God, redeemed by Christ and destined for eternal life, and the secular anthropology that regards us as autonomous, self-regulating individuals. The Catholic perspective regards us as indebted people who receive all that we have as a gratuitous gift of a loving God. The secular view regards us as self-made and guided by an ethic of self-interest. Catholics are a purposeful people who seek the Kingdom in this life and its fullness when we die. Happiness in the here and now is not its primary goal. The secular perspective regards this life as all that there is and enjoying it to the full as an imperative. It is perhaps rather surprising that Catholics fit so seamlessly into contemporary society.

For many people the Church is an irrelevance. They do not believe in God and they do not consider themselves in need of redemption. Others believe in God and may feel that they are part of something greater than themselves but disparage formal religion which they regard as out of touch with the realities of life in the modern world.

Changing cultural norms and attitudes is not easy, particularly in a globalised world. However, they do change over time, as history demonstrates. The attitudes and values of one generation are not always those of the next. The personal and ecclesial renewal that has already been mentioned has the potential to influence cultural attitudes. If Catholics become more confident and able to articulate their own worldview, then that will have an impact more widely. If the joy of the Gospel is evident in our lives, if we live what we profess, embracing all the corporal acts of mercy and reaching out to the poor and the marginalised unequivocally, then people cannot fail to take notice. If our churches are places where there is welcome and communion, guided by pastors who share a common understanding of what it means to be a Catholic, then they will become beacons of hope in an uncertain world. If our Church lives what it preaches and can no longer be accused of disunity and hypocrisy, then it will be taken more seriously by other people.

There also needs to be a serious study of cultural attitudes with a view to seeing how the Gospel can interact with them and influence them. Much academic work in this field already exists but it needs to be brought together and analysed. The challenge here is not to simply dismiss attitudes that do not correspond to a Catholic worldview but rather to dialogue with them and explore whether a shared understanding is beneficial to both the culture and the Church. Consideration must be given to how we inhabit the web and become witnesses in that electronic marketplace.

What is called for here is ambitious. It requires no less than a transformation of our culture from within as we strive to build a Kingdom of "fraternity, justice, peace and dignity"[21] and in so doing become a sign of hope in the Kingdom, which is still to come. Working for the coming of the Kingdom is not something that we can delegate but is intrinsic to a follower of Christ.

Conclusion

What I am suggesting here is that initiatives aimed at personal renewal will not achieve the desired results with regards to evangelisation unless we reform our Church and re-engage and repair our culture. Personal renewal is commendable and an important first step, but that is not enough. The Church needs to be credible both in terms of practising what it preaches and being relevant in the modern world. Cultural dispositions need to be better understood in order to provide a receptive soil for the seed that we sow.

Endnotes

1. *LG*, n. 8.
2. *EN*, n. 26.
3. *EG*, n. 3.
4. Cf. *EN*, n. 54.
5. Cf. ibid., n. 19.
6. Cf. ibid., n. 76.
7. Cf. *EG*, n. 4.
8. Cf. *LG*, n. 1.
9. *EG*, n. 6.
10. Cf. *EN*, n. 22.
11. Cf. ibid., nn. 8 & 13.
12. Cf. *EG*, n. 31.
13. *AA*, n. 3.
14. Cf. *EG*, n. 21.
15. Cf. ibid., n. 24.
16. ibid.
17. ibid., n. 49.
18. ibid., n. 194.
19. Cf. ibid., n. 198.
20. Cf. *EN*, n. 71.
21. *EG*, n. 180.

Chapter Fourteen

Moral Theology: What Happened to Sin?

A Sinful People

Whatever happened to sin? When I was young, we were constantly reminded that we were sinful people and that we had to confess our sins regularly, being clear that if we died in a state of mortal sin we would be condemned. The Penny Catechism told us that mortal sin was "a grievous offence against God", which, "kills the soul and deserves hell". A venial sin "is an offence which does not kill the soul, yet displeases God, and often leads to mortal sin." However, "it is more easily pardoned."[1] The Council of Trent taught that we should confess our sins, relating their number and kind.

After Vatican II, talk of sin disappeared. In contrast to the pre-conciliar admonitions about our sinfulness, we were encouraged to be holy. The word 'sin' was rarely heard. When I interviewed twenty-five Catholic headteachers about their dominant religious motifs in 2011, only two mentioned sin, one whilst explaining what the majority of pupils did during a service of reconciliation whilst others were 'confessing their sins', and the other suggesting that she could not imagine leaving the Church and not just because it would be a 'mortal sin'.

The Catechism of the Catholic Church now talks about sin as "an offense against reason, truth, and right conscience" and a failure of genuine love for

God and neighbour.[2] An interesting change of emphasis here from 'an offence against God' to 'a failure in love of God'. Mortal sin "destroys charity in the heart of man" and "turns man away from God." Venial sin "allows charity to subsist, even though it offends and wounds it."[3] Sin was a failure to obey. Now it is a failure to love.

Enduring Influences

In the Church before Vatican II moral theology was shaped by penitential manuals that provided guidance for confessors on the severity and appropriate penances for sins. The emphasis here was on avoiding sin rather than nurturing virtue, and the focus was on individual acts detached from other aspects of a person's life.[4] We were discouraged from making excuses because of our particular circumstances. Sin was objective, out there, real, and not to be dismissed because of how we perceived what we had done or because we did not think that something was wrong, even though the Church said that it was.

Natural law thinking was, and remains, deeply rooted in the Catholic tradition. It holds that certain principles are built into the human condition. They are inherent in the nature of things and can be discovered by the use of reason. The assertion is that God is the source of natural law and has inscribed his moral law in nature and in man. Acting contrary to the natural law is a sin.

Another recurring theme is that of conscience, an inner voice that calls us to do what is good and avoid what is wrong. The emphasis on conscience has changed over the years. We were always taught to examine our conscience, but this meant recalling when we had failed to be obedient to the Church. Guidance for children perhaps, but many never progressed beyond it. We are now told to discern what is right and, above all, to follow our conscience. However, we are taught that a well-formed conscience will never contradict the objective moral law as taught by Christ and his Church.[5]

Arguably, the influence of St Augustine continues into the present day. St Thomas Aquinas was influenced by Augustine as was the Council of Trent and Vatican II. Augustine's understanding of original sin, through which human nature was impaired resulting in lust and ignorance, has had a lasting impact on the Church's moral teaching in general and its teaching on sexuality in particular.

Another legacy of Augustine that has filtered down to the present day is his maxim that God does not ask us to do what is impossible but makes his grace available to help us. We may find it difficult to follow the moral guidance of the Church, but God will give us the strength to endure, if we pray sincerely for it. This is regarded as 'a central moral and pastoral principle in moral theology in general and in the Church's moral teaching'.[6]

Nineteenth-Century Developments

During the late nineteenth and into the twentieth century new challenges faced moral theology. The world wars and atomic weapons raised issues that the manualists could not answer. People began to ask whether we could ignore history or were we shaped by it. The classicist worldview that everything is ordered as God wants it to be, began to be challenged by a historicist view that the world is constantly developing, and God's plan is only gradually revealed.

The "turn to the subject",[7] the awareness that the person who did the knowing was easier to study than the object of their endeavours, called into question whether it was possible to consider objective truth without taking the subject into account. This subjective turn has schooled us to accept the validity of personal perception and the 'situationality' of moral judgements. Accordingly, only I can decide whether what I did was wrong because only I know my motivation, the relevant circumstances and what I intended the consequences to be. As a result, it is not possible to judge any action to be 'always' wrong. Some broad principles can guide our choices, but individual actions have to be set in context. For example, murder is always wrong, but I can take a life to defend myself and my family.

Gradually, some moral theologians began to consider the person as a whole, and attention moved away from a singular consideration of individual actions. Nature, the essence of what it meant to be human that underpinned natural law, began to be criticised as an abstraction and unrelated to the actual lived experience of the human person. It was argued that sin cannot be contrary to a natural law that does not exist. Neither can anything be defined as 'intrinsically evil' because there is no 'nature' for the evil to offend against 'intrinsically'.

The end of the nineteenth century saw developments in the understanding of the subconscious and heredity. For some these cast doubts on individual culpability. If our sins were a result of forces beyond our control, then surely our guilt was diminished. Indeed, if our thoughts and deeds were not freely chosen, then were they sins at all?

New Approaches

The new emphasis on Scripture, following Vatican II, saw a recognition that in the New Testament it is not Law but love that is the central ethical concept. Love of God and love of neighbour sums up the decalogue. This is underpinned by relationships. Augustine considered sin to be 'contrary to the eternal law', but the Catechism sees sin primarily as "failure in genuine love for God and neighbour."[8] Sin, as so defined, is essentially a failure to love. God does not demand obedience to his law but invites us into a loving relationship. Our response should be to live our lives in gratitude to God and find ways of demonstrating our love.

The emphasis on love as the moral principle that underpins relationships led to the development of situation ethics.[9] If our actions are motivated by unconditional love—a desire to do what is best for the other person—then surely, its protagonist argued, moral principles can be set aside in particular situations.

Somehow, the word 'sin' did not seem to adequately describe failures in relationships. Perhaps the word had become too clearly associated with disobedience to a law. We acknowledged the deficiencies in our relationships at all levels but somehow did not regard them as sinful. Relationships were always prone to misunderstandings and errors of judgement, and we did not believe that we could change that.[10]

Some moral theologians argued that sin should only be attributed to a fundamental rejection of God's offer of a relationship. They argue that individual actions are only sinful if they are the result of this fundamental rejection of God.[11] We all have a basic, God-given disposition to do what we consider to be good. When we genuinely do what we believe to be good, we are responding positively to God's call. This positive response reflects our fundamental option.[12] This changes the individual from a critic into a player. The player has first-hand experience of the game and a direct connection with it. For the player, saying yes to God is not an academic or abstract concept. This 'yes' is lived out in the 'yes' that we say to the earth of which we are stewards, to life which is God's gift to us and to our neighbour through whom we encounter Christ himself.[13]

There has been a growing recognition that unjust structures, which are accepted as the norm, can create an environment where sin is more likely to occur. Although it may be argued that culpability is reduced because the structures place constraints on individual freedom of choice: freedom of choice being a prerequisite of sin.

Magisterial Teaching

Against a backdrop of approaches to morality that challenged traditional Catholic models, Pope St John Paul II promulgated the encyclical *Veritatis Splendor*.[14] The encyclical was written to answer doubts and objections to the Church's moral teaching. The late Pope is particularly concerned with what he perceives as the rift between human freedom and truth, arguing that authentic freedom is intimately connected to truth. Being genuinely free implies embracing truth. He reaffirms that natural law has a universal and permanent character. It is not to be dismissed as an abstraction. Conscience must be informed by reflecting on the natural law and the teaching of the Church. Faith cannot be separated from specific moral imperatives as what we regard as right or wrong, good or bad, is influenced by what we believe. The encyclical rejects any separation between a "fundamental option"[15] and individual acts. Individual acts can change the fundamental option and a manifestation of it. He accepts that intentions and consequences should be taken into account but insists that it is the act itself that is of central importance. He affirms that some kinds of behaviour are opposed to truth and human nature and are "intrinsically evil."[16]

Advocates of the encyclical see it as a necessary corrective to widespread dissent and a rebuttal of those who argue that there are no acts that are always wrong. Even some of its critics recognise strengths in the encyclical. It affirms objectivity in moral thinking as an antidote to relativism. It stresses the link between moral theology and faith, between the moral life and religious commitment. In other words, you can't separate moral decision making from the teaching of the Church.

Critics of *Veritatis Splendor* argue that it adopts a classicist view of the world and ignores the historicism that has been the main feature of theology since Vatican II.[17] They contend that presenting moral issues from a legal view point goes against a scriptural, Christ-centred perspective, where love not law is the currency and we are invited to respond to God's offer of a loving relationship.

So, Where Does That Leave Sin?

When sin was disobedience to divine rules, underpinned by natural law and taught by the Church, it was easy to identify. If you broke the rule, you sinned. It was a sin to miss Mass on Sunday. There may be extenuating circumstance such as serious illness, but you were still obliged to confess the offence and let the priest decide whether there was sufficient mitigation. Some sins were minor, venial, but others were more serious, and some were mortal, they caused spiritual death.

In the early Church, it was only mortal sins that needed to be confessed and so people were not expected to make a confession more than once in their lifetime. Gradually, the practice of regular confession encouraged people to offer a catalogue of minor, often repeated, offences. If my fundamental option is to say 'yes' to God even though I do things wrong because of the weakness of the human condition, then I commit no mortal sin. If I only have to confess mortal sins, then I have no need of confession.

There is a danger that modern developments in moral thinking contribute to anomie and a dystopian future where sin no longer has any meaning. Against this tendency, the Church stresses the community aspects of morality based on principles derived from the Scriptures. It denies any dichotomy between freedom and truth or faith and morality. It prioritises conscience but insists that it must be formed by the teaching of the Church.

The Debate Continues

The letter to bishops from the Congregation for the Doctrine of the Faith (CDF), *Placuit Deo*, warns against losing sight of sin—a warning echoed by Pope Francis in his Exhortation *Gaudete Et Exsultate*.[18] It reminds us of the old Pelagian heresy that we are essentially good and can achieve salvation by our own efforts. Sin is real, the CDF reminds us, and it is only by the grace of God that we can overcome the weakness of the human condition. We receive that grace primarily through the Sacraments and, in this context, through the Sacrament of Reconciliation.[19]

The tension between culture and Church teaching is acknowledged by the CDF.[20] These tensions are also made explicit by Pope Francis in his Exhortation *Amoris Laetitia*. Whilst affirming traditional teaching that something that is objectively wrong remains so, regardless of the circumstances, he draws on the catechism to argue that culpability can be diminished by many factors.[21] There is a need to recognise that a given situation can be complex[22] and this must be taken into account when judging the degree of culpability of individuals.[23]

These tensions are manifest in the family, the parish and the school. In fact, in any situation where Church teaching is explained and defended. There would still seem to be much to do to inform our consciences and reconcile our lived experience with Church teaching.

Endnotes

1   *The Explanatory Catechism of Christian Doctrine*, (London: Burns & Oates, 1921), Answers 121,122,126 & 127.

2   CCC, n. 1849.

3   ibid., n. 1855.

4   T.E. O'Connell, 'The History of Moral Theology', in M. Hayes and L. Gearon (eds.), *Contemporary Catholic Theology: A Reader*, (New York: Continuum, 2000), p. 393.

5   Cf. CCC, nn. 1783-5, 1792, 2039.

6   J. Mahoney, *The Making of Moral Theology: A Study of the Roam Catholic Tradition*, (Oxford: Clarendon Press, 1987), p. 53.

7   J.F. Keenan, *A History of Catholic Moral Theology in the Twentieth Century: From Confessing Sins to Liberating Consciences*, (London & New York: Continuum, 2010), p. 35.

8   CCC, n. 1849.

9   Cf. J. Fletcher, *Situation ethics: The new morality*, (Louisville, KY, Westminster: John Knox Press, 1997).

10   Cf. J.F. Keenan, 'Raising expectations of Sin' in *Theological Studies* Vol. 77(1) (2016), p. 172.

11   Cf. R. Egan, 'Epistemological Foundations for a Theology of Sin' in *The Heythrop Journal*, LVII (2016), p. 558.

12   Mahoney, *The Making of Moral Theology*, p. 121.

13   S. Fegan, *What happened to Sin*, (Dublin: The Columba Press, 2008).

14   Cf. W.M. Maina, 'The Shaping of Moral Theology: *Veritatis Splendor* and the Debate of the Nature of Roman Catholic Moral Theology' in *Journal for the Study of Religions and Ideologies*, vol. 12, issue 35(2013), pp. 178–221.

15   Pope St John Paul II, *Veritatis Splendor*, (Vatican website, 1993), n. 65.

16   ibid., n. 67.

17   C.E. Curran, *The Catholic Moral Tradition—a Synthesis*, (Washington DC: Georgetown University Press, 1999), p. 147.

18   Cf. Pope Francis, *Gaudete et Exsultate* (Vatican website, 2018).

19   Cf. CDF, Letter *Placuit Deo* (Vatican website, 2018).

20   *Placuit Deo*, n. 2.

21   Cf. Pope Francis, *Amoris Laetitia*, (Vatican website 2017) [*AL*], n. 302, and CCC, n. 1735.

22   *AL*, n. 296.

23   ibid., n. 302.

CHAPTER FIFTEEN

The Catholic School Landscape

Introduction

Catholic schools play a significant role in the provision of education in England and Wales. They are popular and successful. However, even though the landscape within which they operate may not be hostile, neither is it benign. The terrain that bishops and headteachers have to negotiate is challenging, and it is perhaps a useful exercise to try and outline some of the cultural, ecclesial and personal obstacles around which they must manoeuvre.

Cultural Challenges

The cultural climate is unsupportive of faith. Increasing numbers of people claim to have no religion. This appears to be getting worse generation by generation.[1] The media tends to treat religious belief as quaint at best, more often ridiculous and at worst harmful. The demise of rational analysis and its replacement by emotions as an arbiter of values and guide to actions means that whatever makes me feel okay, is okay. This is fuelled by a cynical disregard for truth as a standard to be defended and a decline into relativism where one opinion, however uninformed, has the same weight as any other.

Many adults who were baptised and raised as Catholics claim to have no religious affiliation.[2] This disaffiliation no doubt has many causes. Among them are the cultural climate which is increasingly secular; political expediency favouring populist agendas, some of which are in direct conflict with the teaching of the Church; the rise of popular consensus and reflection on personal narratives as sources of legitimacy; a decline in respect for the wisdom of age; an escalating generation gap fuelled in part by electronic communication; and the disavowal of value judgements in a pluralist society.

All this is important because the baptised, including teachers and students, are not immune to the spirit of the age. Their own worldview is influenced by what they see and hear around them. This can lead to tensions between what the Church teaches and what they actually believe.

Competing Catholic Theologies

The plethora of theological approaches that arose after Vatican II encourages a more individualistic interpretation of Church teaching. Conflicting theological approaches surfaced at the synod on the family in 2015. One approach tends to rely on truths of faith deduced from Revelation using philosophical techniques. From this perspective, nothing changes. The truth cannot alter. There is an emphasis on the transcendence of God, the divinity of Christ, the authority of the *Magisterium*, as well as on the ordained clergy and canon law. This approach is sometimes seen as *Kerygmatic* or a 'theology from above'. The other approach tends to see truth as organic and arising from experience. From this perspective, doctrine must develop as our understanding of it increases. There is an emphasis on the imminence of God, the humanity of Jesus, the legitimacy of the *sensus fidei* and human experience. This is sometimes regarded as existential, or as a 'theology from below'.

These theological approaches are not mutually exclusive but, as became evident following the post-synodal exhortation *Amoris Laetitia*, they can lead to different interpretations, and judgements about what is compatible with the Catholic tradition. This can cause problems for schools both in discerning what they should teach and managing competing expectations from local clergy and parishioners.

Perspectives on Catholic Schools

A feature of the landscape that complicates matters is the diverse and often divergent opinions that exist about the nature and purpose of Catholic schools, even within the Catholic sector. At the most fundamental level, there is the debate about the place of evangelisation and catechesis within the Catholic school. Some will argue that there is no place for these in a national education system and that we risk the good will of legislators by insisting on them. Others find it hard to understand what point there is to a Catholic school that does not expose its pupils to the Gospel or help believers to gain a better understanding of their faith.

There are a variety of views on the balance to be struck between what might be called communion and mission. 'Communion' here refers to those features that are 'distinctively Catholic' and find expression in forms that stress the importance of the integrity of the Catholic community, and 'mission' to those features that concentrate on the duty to reach out to those beyond itself.

The tendency of the communion-orientated school is to offer a safe haven for Catholic doctrine and practice. Admission arrangements favour committed practising Catholic families, and the presence of pupils who do not share the Catholic faith is seen as a potential threat to the integrity of the school. The unspoken assumption is that the majority of pupils are believing Catholics whose faith should be nurtured.

The tendency of the mission-orientated school is to engage with a broken society and contribute to its healing by promoting a Catholic understanding of the common good. They welcome pupils who are not Catholics and celebrate their contribution to the school. An unspoken assumption here is that it is possible to find a contemporary language of faith that will inspire a new generation.

In Catholic schools, which privilege 'communion,' policy and practice are influenced by their Catholic 'confessional' orientation. In schools, which privilege 'mission,' then policy and practice will be influenced by a desire for dialogue and engagement with the world outside the Church. To these it is possible to add a third, which might be called 'residual'. In a 'residual' Catholic school policy and practice are primarily influenced by pressures and horizons that do not depend on any confessional orientation for their legitimacy. In a sense, schools that emphasise 'communion' see themselves as bringing Christ to the world. Schools that emphasise 'mission' are engaged in finding Christ in the word. 'Residual' Catholic schools are concerned to offer a sound secular education with Christ in the background.

Some Catholic schools can be identified with each of these types but most combine elements of each.

Objections to Catholic Schools

Catholic schools are opposed by some sections of the community who object to all 'faith schools', either on ideological grounds because they reject religious belief as irrational and illiberal, or because of a fear of radicalisation. They refuse to accept that it is as rational to believe as not to believe, and that it is difficult to appreciate our literature and culture without an understanding of Christianity. They ignore the long and seminal influence of Catholic education in this country and the absence of radicalisation in our schools.

These and numerous other criticisms can all be answered, but in this post-truth age, the fact that they are made gives them credence. Catholic school leaders will argue that they make a positive contribution to society, helping to raise academic standards, enhance community cohesion, encourage positive attitudes and behaviour amongst pupils, as well as making an economic contribution to society. In addition, there is no evidence that Catholic schools cause harm.[3]

There is a popular view that religion is a private matter and should not be given a platform in the public arena. This pervasive line of thought implies that a person can detach religious belief from the rest of their life.[4] It denies implicitly any connection between what we believe and the moral judgements that we make. Indeed, a moral judgement that can be traced back to a religious belief is to be summarily rejected regardless of its rational credentials.

There has been pressure on government for some time to insist that 'faith schools' include a cross section of students from many faith traditions and none. In part this is driven by a fear of sectarianism or at least the divisiveness of segregated communities. It has also been argued that if Catholics think their schools are of such a benefit to society, then they should be open to all. Some Catholic educators are inclined to accept these arguments. However, the Catholic community has historically invested large amounts of money in its schools so that Catholic parents can have their children educated in accordance with their beliefs which, rather than being antithetical to British values, are, in fact, their seed bed. It is difficult to turn away Catholic families from our schools in order to give places to those from outside the Church.

Another problem associated with this arises from the shortage of Catholic teachers. In an environment where the majority of the staff are committed Catholics such as was the case in schools run by religious orders, then it was possible to maintain a Catholic environment even when Catholic students were in a minority. With a reduced number of Catholic staff and the lack of practice of many Catholic students, this is more problematic. There is a serious concern that our schools would become 'residual' as described above.

Challenges from Within

Even within the Catholic Church there are criticisms of Catholic schools. The decline in Church attendance and the apparent lack of religious literacy among the faithful are blamed on the schools. Surely, it is argued, we can spend our money more efficiently on programmes of evangelisation that will bear more fruit. I have never really understood the appeal of this argument. Where else are we going to be provided with the opportunity to expose large numbers of young people to the Gospel?

There may be deficiencies in Catholic schools, and these must constantly be kept under review. However, a critical problem faced by the Church that does not originate from their schools is the gap between what is taught and what is believed. This was identified by the theologian Karl Rahner over twenty-five years ago and is not showing any signs of closing.[5] On the whole, schools work hard to bridge what is often a chasm, but the competing Catholic theologies exacerbate the problem.

Philosophical and Pragmatic Challenges to Catholic Schools

External forces present philosophical and pragmatic challenges for Catholic schools. Contemporary English education is essentially instrumental.[6] It is primarily concerned with preparing people for their role in society, and the indicators of its success, such as examination results, are those that can be measured empirically. Catholic schools are concerned with developing people as people[7] and value aspects of learning, such as spiritual development, which cannot be evaluated using numerical data. The challenge for Catholic schools is to maintain the integrity of their mission[8] within this climate and avoid the temptation to emphasise those elements of what they offer that are valued more generally in society, whilst relegating distinctively Catholic features to the margins, or simply becoming a state school conducted in premises provided by the Catholic Church.[9]

Catholic schools also have to satisfy multiple masters. They must satisfy Ofsted that they are providing a sound secular education and that they are financially viable. They have to satisfy parents that the needs of their individual children are being met. They have to satisfy the diocese of the religious integrity of the school. Each constituency has its own expectations and they are not always readily compatible.

The Young People Themselves

Then there are the students themselves. What do they believe? How confident are they in the Church? Unsurprisingly, they comprise a patchwork of varying beliefs and attitudes. There are those who are committed to the triad of Catholic practice, namely Sunday Mass attendance, personal prayer and action for social justice. There are those who have little or no involvement with the Church or religious practice in general. Others fall in between.[10] On the whole, they are open and approachable, but their underlying assumptions are not those of earlier generations of Catholic students. In many parts of the world, such as Africa, where the community is the central feature of life, the individual sees him or herself as part of that grouping and not separate from it. In Western society, people tend to see themselves as the central character in a drama, sometimes a comedy and sometimes a tragedy, called 'myself'. We no longer look to others for permission to live our lives as we choose.

Children grow up in an environment where they are given choices from an early age and taught that they have rights that other people must respect. This is not only taught to them formally but also learnt from experience. They learn that adults see laws as guidelines not as rules, and that uninformed opinions and mistaken perceptions are valued.

Whether it is because we value experience and feelings over rational arguments or because we have become disillusioned with the state, science or religion as sources of knowledge, society no longer trusts the judgements of a higher authority, and so neither do young people. In a climate of spin, trust becomes problematic. People are often sceptical if not cynical about what they are told by those in authority, including the Church.

Young people are growing up in a society where they do not, on the whole, look for the 'bigger picture'. They look for authenticity and this they only recognise as coming from their own experience and that of their peers. They find security in their own opinions.[11] Clearly, their own knowledge and understanding and that of their immediate friends will place limitations on their interpretation of their experiences.

Although there is evidence of stress and anxiety among young people, it would be a mistake to think that all the young people in our schools are unhappy with their lives. On the whole, they are essentially happy about life and positive about the future. The world is generally seen as a good place and although bad things can happen, these can be managed with the support of family and friends. They do not look for the meaning of life outside the here and now. They accept that they are not perfect but don't consider themselves to be in need of redemption.[12]

The challenge is to reconcile the teaching of the Church, which reflects the experience, thought and prayer of two millennia, but which can often seem alien to young people, with the realities of life as they experience it today.

Conclusion

Such is the landscape within which Catholic schools operate. Indeed, this represents only a snapshot of some aspects of that landscape. Catholic schools are on the frontline in the battle for the hearts, minds and souls of young people. The cultural climate is contentious, the ecclesial environs equivocal, the disposition of the students sceptical and the future unpredictable. If we are to proclaim the Gospel in the modern world, then we need to find ways of answering contemporary cultural challenges, and before we can hope to do this, we need to heal the divisions that exist within the Catholic Church. This is not a task for the schools. They are pilgrims in an unstable landscape and in need of our prayers and support.

Endnotes

1   A. Crockett & A. Voas, 'Generations of Decline: Religious Change in 20th-Century Britain' in *Journal for the Scientific Study of Religion*, 45(4) (2006), 567–584.

2   S. Bullivant, *Contemporary Catholicism in England and Wales: A statistical report based on recent British Social Attitudes survey data*, (St Mary's University, Twickenham: Benedict XVI Centre for Religion and Society, 2016), p. 11.

3   For other objections and their refutations see A.B. Morris, *Fifty Years On: The Case for Catholic Schools*, (Chelmsford: Matthew James Publishing, 2008), pp. 33–50.

4   Cf. F. Campbell, 'On Catholic Education and Integrity' in R. Convery, L. Franchi & R. McCluskey (eds.), *Reclaiming the Piazza II: Catholic Education and the New Evangelisation*, (Leominster: Gracewing, 2017).

5   K Rahner, *Theological Investigations: Vol XXII Humane Society and the Church of Tomorrow*, (New York: Crossroads, 1991), p. 113.

6   Cf. R. Pring, 'Markets Education and Catholic Schools' in McLaughlin et al. (eds.), *The Contemporary Catholic School: Context, Identity and Diversity*, (Washington: Falmer, 1996), p. 57–69. Also see A. Price, 'Turbulent Times—A Challenge to Catholic Education in Britain Today' in Conroy (ed.), *Catholic Education: Inside-Out and Outside-In*, pp. 112-134.

7   See Conroy, '"The Long Johns" and Catholic Education', p. 47.

8   Grace, *Catholic Schools: Mission, Markets and Morality*, pp. 178, 235 & 237.

9   Treston, 'Ethos and identity: Foundational concerns for Catholic schools', p. 17.

10   Cf. D. Curtin & S. Davies, *Complex Catholicism: Discovering the reality of young Catholics; A Detailed Typology*, (London: Camino House & CYMFED, 2018).

11   Cf. R. Scruton, *The West and the Rest: Globalisation and the Terrorist Threat*, (New York: Continuum International Press, 2002), p. 75.

12   Cf. Savage, et al., *Making Sense of Generation Y*.

CHAPTER SIXTEEN

Leadership of Service: Letting Go

A Desire to Serve

The synoptic gospels all recount the same incident where a dispute arises among the apostles about status (Mk 10:35-45, Matt 20:25-28, Lk 22:24-27). Individual details differ, but all three accounts resonate with human experience in general and ecclesial history down the ages. The desire for status and with it the right to exercise authority over others seems to be hardwired into the human condition. The answer that Jesus gives in all three Gospels redefines hierarchy, 'whoever wants to be first must be your slave'. In Luke's account this is illustrated by insisting that the leader must be the one who serves at table not the one who is served.

John does not recount this particular incident but provides a powerful model wherein Jesus practices what he preached by insisting that he wash the feet of his disciples (Jn 13:1-15). Having completed this task Jesus mandates those who will go on to lead the Church to 'copy what I have done'. Status is not enhanced by sitting in a place of honour but by providing service for the community, even demeaning oneself for the sake of others. This is not a leadership by those who wish to be greeted obsequiously in the street and be addressed with a special title (cf. Matt 23:6). It is the leadership of those whose desire is to serve.

An Elite Cast

This is sometimes called servant leadership and it is not easy to describe or to practise. For priests it is a particular challenge. It is difficult for them to avoid feeling special, superior in many ways to their lay brethren. They have undergone a long period of formation, which included immersing themselves in the Scriptural, theological, liturgical and juridical tradition of the Church. They have been invested with a supernatural power and are called to act *in persona Christi capitis*. They share in the bishop's ministry of teaching, sanctifying and governing. In most cases, they have committed themselves to celibacy and live a life dedicated to prayer and worship and the pastoral care of their community.

The laity are complicit in fostering this sense of superiority by treating priests with an exaggerated level deference and respect. The priest's word is often taken as 'gospel' even when others have a better grasp of the matter at hand. This can encourage an understanding of service as something that the priest provides; something that the priest does for the people. If there was such a thing as a professional Christian, he would be it and, like other professionals, would provide a service based on his training and experience. Surely, he knows what the people need.

Being a member of such an elite cast mitigates against the humility required to be a servant leader. Despite this, many priests are humble men, who do see servant leadership in terms of 'walking with' people—supporting, encouraging and guiding them. Here they face the challenges that all who try to exercise servant leadership experience. How to lead from within rather than from the front? These challenges are exacerbated by trying to lead a cluster of parishes or a single parish with multiple churches and communities. They face the anxiety of all leaders that it will descend into chaos if they lose control.

I want to offer some thoughts on the nature of servant leadership and how it can be exercised in a large parish without everything descending into chaos.

Servant Leadership

Servant leadership is a leadership of loving service. It is *agape*, an unselfish love, but also *caritas*, a love that is received from God and given to others.

There is a danger in defining servant leadership in this way. It can lead to a paternalistic approach, a sort of benevolent despotism with the concomitant, even if unintended, infantilisation of the laity. Jesus didn't tell his apostles to lead with compassion and kindness, with a fatherly concern for their people, with justice even. Rather, their service was to be modelled on his own, which was a total commitment to service of the washing of feet, serving at table kind. This requires humility and self-sacrifice.[1]

It is probably a mistake to think of servant leadership as one of many approaches to leadership that can be deployed depending on circumstances. Management theorists will be familiar with leadership typologies such as autocratic, persuasive, consultative or democratic.[2] Unlike these, servant leadership is not a tool to be deployed when required. Like a virtue it is dispositional. It can't be taught, but it can be acquired given appropriate formation. Once embraced it informs all the leader's work and witness.

For Catholics there is a clear duty to have a particular concern for the weak and marginalised. The servant leader is someone who tries to remove inequalities and promote social justice. He is also able to encourage the least prominent members of the parish, helping them to feel that they are valued within the community.[3]

Servant leaders want to release the potential in each person; to identify and nurture their God-given talents: to discern the part that the Holy Spirit is calling each one to play. Releasing, identifying, nurturing and discerning are among the indicators of genuine servant leadership. This is not about empowering others, giving them the skills and authority to act, rather it is about enabling others, removing barriers that prevent them being all that they are called to be, fully alive we might say (Jn 10:10). The servant priest seeks "the glory of God resplendent in his people, alive and strengthened."[4]

Levels of Involvement

In order to explore how this can be managed in practice, I want to borrow from the work of Jeanne Wilson and her colleagues.[5] It suggest a continuum of levels of involvement by a leader. Before describing it, I should say that I operated according to this model when I was a headteacher, as indeed did others, and so it cannot be dismissed as pure theory. I would also like to acknowledge that there is always some reticence to adopt approaches which have been developed in a secular setting. The Church is, we must remember, "a reality imbued with the hidden presence of God."[6] Consequently, I think of decision-making in the parish as a process of discernment. It should be done prayerfully and in the light of the Gospel. Clearly not all decision-making is of this kind but in what follows I assume that important decision-making is.

Command and Control

At one end of the continuum, the priest is in sole command. Everyone else reports to him and seeks his approval before taking any significant decision. This allows the priest to satisfy himself that everything is remaining orthodox, as he sees it, and that he is exercising his fiduciary duty to the bishop. He may feel that he is protecting the parish from ginger groups and 'false prophets'. This gives him maximum control and can be a useful starting point because it can help to overcome inertia and gets things done. The danger with this approach is that it encourages parishioners to become 'passive' recipients of what is provided for them. It fails to nurture responsibility for sustaining and developing the parish. It limits the scope for others to make the best use of their talents. It denies the parish a wealth of experience and creativity. It also places a heavy burden on the priest as the complexity of the parish grows.

At a more subtle level, this approach fails to tap into the informal system of relationships that always operates in a parish.[7] It can result in people who actually know how things work being marginalised and left without a voice. Although it is not always good practice to blindly continue along an already determined path, most wise leaders try to learn from the previous experiences of the parish.

It is possible for a priest to operate in this way and genuinely see himself as a servant leader. After all, he is working for the good of others, not himself. He gives unstintingly of his time and energy, often feeling physically and emotionally drained. He does treat people with respect and, in a sense, acts as a conduit for the love of God. However, as he clearly thinks that only he can keep the parish on an even course, a question arises about the depth of his humility. The humility required of the servant leader is not just at the level of interpersonal behaviour and a willingness to do some of the messy jobs. It involves renouncing any claim to a monopoly of wisdom and holiness and risking letting go.

Letting Go

Further along the continuum we find a move towards 'participative' leadership. The priest still appoints helpers, resolves disputes and makes key decisions; however, he involve others in problem-solving, encourages them to recommend improvements and develops a two-way system of communication. Gradually other parishioners take on aspects of leadership and are allowed the discretion to lead teams and make decisions on their own. Wilson suggest that it is often at this point that the leader begins to feel vulnerable and disinclined to share leadership more fully. It is a time in the parish's life for catechesis and adult formation more generally. Lay ministers have to be trained and people have to be encouraged to develop their understanding of the tradition, to grow in their faith you might say.

Further along still, the priest has become one among equals. He sees himself as 'in the parish' not just 'out in front of the parish'. Leadership has been distributed widely and the main areas of parish life and involvement are directed by lay people. Decision-making is enhanced by greater participation in it and rather than relying on known capabilities, new approaches are encouraged with flexibility and creativity highly valued. The priest could be absent for a few weeks and, with the obvious exception of Confession and Eucharist, everything would carry on as normal.

By the time we reach the other end of the continuum, the priest is able to leave most of the parish administration to others and can use his time more effectively on pastoral and Sacramental activities. In a sense he now stands slightly outside the main parish decision-making mechanisms and can act as an adviser with a holistic overview.

There are difficulties associated with this more distributed approach to leadership. Consultation and collaboration can be slow and ineffective. Accountability is more complex. There is a danger that people will pursue their own pet projects to the detriment of a more common purpose. It also requires a willingness on the part of the laity to engage in regular and sustained formation so that decision making is informed by Church teaching and not just personal preferences.

Recognising the Context

It must be remembered that all leadership takes place in a particular context. It is always situational. A new parish priest must judge the developmental stage of the parish before distributing leadership too widely. At the same time, he must begin the process of developing the knowledge and skills of parishioners, if these are deficient. He must make use of existing talents to sustain current practice whilst nurturing new untapped talent with which to move the parish forward.

Keeping It Together

As leadership is distributed more widely, the priest remains accountable in canon law for the health of the community that he serves. How is he to ensure the continued vitality and integrity of the parish when he no longer has his hands on all the levers of power? My answer to this is to create a framework within which everyone is expected to operate. This may take the form of a list of key principles that inform how we do things around here. In a school setting I started with a list of key principles that I asked my senior staff to expand and amend. Once we had a comprehensive list, we began the process of amalgamating and editing until we had only ten key principles. These we consulted on more widely, amended further and finally adopted as our framework.

In a parish this may take a different form. It is common practice for parishes to develop some kind of mission statement with key aims.[8] These shape the future direction of the parish. The process of arriving at this statement and aims is as important as the outcome. It is essential that parishioners discuss and assimilate the aim. This then becomes the framework within which people can exercise discretion in their various leadership roles. The priest has to meet with those in key roles to ensure that they are still being faithful to the agreed mission. This is what prevents the parish losing focus and fragmenting.

Keeping Faithful

Throughout this whole process, the integrity of the priest is paramount. As I have already suggested, the default setting of most Catholics is to trust their priest. Openness and transparency, never a strong suit in the Catholic Church, is a prerequisite of maintaining that trust. Nuancing conversations to bring different people on board is an advanced skill but giving contradictory messages erodes trust. If parishioners don't trust their priest, they will not follow him enthusiastically and without followers, what kind of leader is he?

One stumbling block to be avoided is the temptation to overrule someone in a leadership position in response to an appeal from another parishioner. This must be managed sensitively whilst maintaining the integrity of the distributed leadership network. If people believe that they can bypass those with leadership responsibilities, then they will, and the system in undermined.

Challenge and Reward

The kind of servant leadership advocated here requires prayer, patience and professionalism. It is challenging but rewarding. I was interested to note that the essential elements of what I have proposed here can be identified in Fr Mallon's book 'Divine Renovation',[9] which has been recommended in many dioceses as a blueprint for renewal.

Endnotes

1   K. Punnachet, 'Catholic servant-leadership in education: going beyond the secular paradigm' in *International Studies in Catholic Education*, Vol. 1, No. 2, October (2009), pp. 117–134.

2   R. Tannenbaum, & W.H. Schmidt, 'How to choose a leadership pattern', *The Harvard Business Review*, May-June (1973), pp. 162–180.

3   Cf. P.G. Northouse, *Leadership: Theory and Practice*, 5th edition, (London: Sage, 2010), p.385.

4   Pope Francis Homily, Chrism Mass (2013).

5   J.M. Wilson, J. George, R.S. Wellins & W.C. Byham, *Leadership Trapeze: Strategies for Leadership in Team-based Organisations* (San Francisco, Jossey-Bass, 1994).

6   Pope Paul VI: Opening address at second session of Vatican II.

7   C. Heckscher, 'Defining the Post-Bureaucratic Type', in C. Heckscher & A. Donnellon (eds.), *The Post-Bureaucratic Organisation: new perspectives on organisational change.* (Newbury Park, CA: Sage, 1994), p. 21.

8   It is beyond the scope of this short article to explore 'mission' more fully.

9   J. Mallon, *Divine Renovation: Bringing your Parish from Maintenance to Mission*, (New London, CT: Twenty Third Publications, 2014).

CHAPTER SEVENTEEN

Ordinary Catholic Theology

Retrieving Theology

In the first of a series of articles in 'The Pastoral Review', Professor O'Loughlin posed the question "Why study theology?"[1] He acknowledged that it was sometimes seen as dry and boring, the preserve of academics and clergy, but insisted that it also had relevance for the non-academic, not theologically trained, Christian, who we might regard as an 'ordinary believer'. Helpfully, O'Loughlin suggested that theology was less like physics, which we could ignore whilst still benefitting from its insights, and more like cooking, at which we improve with training.

My aim here is to suggest another dimension of theology that plays a part in all our lives whether we recognise it or not and whether we are trained in theology or not. This is what Jeff Astley called 'ordinary theology'.[2] Now, I need to be clear at the outset that it is not my intention to disparage academic theology. Clearly it plays an essential role in providing a rational basis for our faith and helping to clarify what is meant by the fundamental questions about life and death that present themselves to all people. What I want to suggest is that not only should we regard theology as a servant not the substance of the faith but that any effective renewal of the Church requires a retrieval of theology as an everyday function of the Christian life.

Speaking About God

We know that the earliest theology was essentially practical. The Gospels, the letters of Paul and the Apostolic Fathers were largely concerned with the practice of the faith within the community of believers. Apologists recruited contemporary philosophy in defence of the apostolic teachings. As a written Scripture was accepted, this became the bedrock of theology and as it moved from prominent bishops through the monasteries into universities, it became more philosophical and scholarly. St Thomas Aquinas would regard it not as practical but as speculative.

So, theology found its way into the hallowed halls of academia and beyond the reach of the ordinary believer, who was probably unable to grasp its finer points. After all, St Anselm had advised that those who did not understand the teaching of the Church should simply bow their heads in submission. But at its simplest, theology, as the Greek *theologia* indicates, is speaking about God, and this is something that the ordinary believer does frequently. When praying, taking part in the liturgy, engaging in informal discussions, indeed when reaching out to those in need in response to the Lord's command, we are all speaking of God.

I would not want to be understood as claiming that any casual reference to God counts as theology. I would accept that it has to be reflective. It also grows out of faith. St Anselm said theology was "faith seeking understanding"[3] and it is generally accepted that it is the activity of a believer and arises from within a community of believers. Astley regarded ordinary theology as the religious talk of those who had received no formal theological training. He did not regard it as any stream of religious unconsciousness but as a wisdom that arose from the heart of a believer.

For us, the question is, can there be an 'ordinary Catholic theology'. To answer this question, I want to consider the formational environment within which speaking of God is first experienced and the extent to which speaking of God can be seen as an expression of the *sensus fidei*, under the influence of the Holy Spirit.

A Nurturing Catholic Environment

There is little doubt that most Catholics hear their first talk about God from their parents. Indeed, they hear about Jesus before they have any idea that there is such a thing as theology. They learn to pray at home and are initiated into the Sacramental and liturgical life of the parish community. It is within this formational Catholic community that they first learn to express what they believed, to begin to give voice to the hope that is within them.

We are only able to understand theological concepts such as love, forgiveness and sacrifice if we have experienced them ourselves, and it is within the family that we gain these experiences. In this environment, faith is almost taken for granted. It is living the faith that occupies us. Thinking and talking about it are far less important. It is out of this overtly Catholic, if not always strictly orthodox, context that our ordinary Catholic theology develops. It is here that we come to see through the eyes of faith. It is here that we develop what *Lumen Gentium* describes as a "supernatural appreciation of the faith"[4] and calls the *sensus fidei*.

Ordinary Catholic theology is an attempt to give expression to the *sensus fidei*, to articulate what is known intuitively. Now, of course, this does not guarantee the inerrancy of ordinary Catholic theology. Not every opinion, not even every religious opinion is inspired by faith. Other influences play their part, but this does not devalue ordinary theology, which remains an authentic expression of what is actually believed. Two mechanisms safeguard the orthodoxy of ordinary theology. One is the authoritative hierarchy known as the *Magisterium*. The second involves the entire people of God and resides under an apparently simple description: discernment.

Discernment and Magisterium

Discernment requires prayerful reflection and humble dialogue. The outcome of such a process is the faith of the Church what is sometimes called the *sensus fidelium*. The entire People of God are called to engage in the process of discernment. This includes the lowliest lay person as well as the most eminent bishop. In a sense the meaning of the individual expressions of faith can only be understood in the light of the whole teaching of the Church and, paradoxically, the whole teaching of the Church can only be understood in the light of the individual expressions of faith. Guided by the Holy Spirit this discernment results in an authoritative expression of faith by the *Magisterium*, who are charged with listening to the Word of God, guarding it and proclaiming it.[5]

Sensus Fidei of All the Baptised

Following Vatican II, no Papal Encyclical or Apostolic Exhortation mentioned the *sensus fidei* until Pope Francis resurrected it in *Evangelii Gaudium*. He asked the International Theological Commission (ITC) to explore its origins and significance. In tracing it through Scripture and tradition, the ITC came to the conclusion that the *sensus fidei* is proportional to one's involvement in the life of faith. In other words, the more fully immersed you are in the life of faith, the more open you are to be guided by the Holy Spirit. However, it noted that insights are given to those of humble faith (cf. Matt 11:25, Lk 10:21) and even the baptised who are not fully committed have aspects of the *sensus fidei* and deserve to be heard.[6] In other words, those who are not fully formed or informed can still have insights arising from the presence of the Holy Spirit in their lives. Essentially what is being asserted is that the ordinary theology of all the baptised is of value.

The Rational and The Intuitive

Rather than dismissing ordinary theology as inadequate the 'New Evangelisation' needs to raise its profile and encourage people to express their faith. Two particular difficulties need to be overcome. First, the assumption that ordinary theology is inferior to academic theology needs to be challenged. The question is about the relative importance of reason and intuition. Is intuition an unruly servant that has to be mastered, or is reason an arrogant child in need of restraint? Shakespeare captured this tension when he wrote that "There are more in heaven and earth, Horatio, than are dreamt of in your philosophy."[7] Likewise, Wittgenstein alluded to it when he noted that science puts us to sleep and we need to awaken to wonder.[8] These, and many other thinkers, recognise the importance of intuition.

Those who study the working of the human brain have come to accept that the rational part of the brain is only able to make use of what it can rationalise. It is constrained by what it already knows and strives to make sense of pieces of a jigsaw of which it has no complete picture. The intuitive part of the brain captures the whole picture but does not attempt to articulate it because it is beyond its capability. The rational part of the brain, which controls language, draws down partial aspects of the whole that is known by the intuitive part. This process has proven helpful for the development of the human capacity to manage its environment, but in losing sight of the whole, it endangers the very environment that it seeks to manage.[9]

Academic theology is a function of the rational part of the brain. It might be argued that it does not see the bigger picture, the full jigsaw, even though it strives to construct it from the fragments that it has gathered. Ordinary theology is the function of the intuitive part of the brain and is necessarily inadequate and only offers glimpses of what it knows. The rational part of the brain is not superior to the intuitive part. Academic theology is not superior to ordinary theology. They are both part of a whole and, to some extent the rational is a servant of the intuitive and academic is a servant of the ordinary.[10] As a footnote to this argument, it should be pointed out that the two parts of the brain do not work independently. Ordinary theology does not abandon all claims to rationality. It is worth recalling that the First Vatican Council decreed that "God... can be known with certitude by the natural light of human reason from created things."[11] There is sometimes an assumption here that the Church will do this reasoning. However, according to Rahner, it is not the Church's competence in this matter that is being asserted but the rational capacity of every person.[12] According to the teaching of the Church therefore, the ordinary theologian can know about the things of God through natural reason and an intuition for the faith.

Adult Formation

The second difficulty to overcome is the need for a comprehensive programme of adult formation that allows people to become more confident in their intuitions and express their faith more fluently. Indeed, it is finding an appropriate language to express deeply held beliefs that is often the main stumbling block for the ordinary believer. Technical theological language is of little help. Listening to how others have made sense of it all can prove very rewarding. The stories that people tell and the metaphors that they use often resonate with something unspoken that resides deep in their listeners' hearts.

Through guided dialogue with other believers and the teaching of the Church, they engage in a process of discernment and come to recognise the value of the contributions that they make as a legitimate expression of the *sensus fidei*. There needs to be encouragement to recognise that they are doing theology because any genuine expression of their faith is theological.[13] It is not important whether what they say is fully in accord with the teaching of the Church. They are not making authoritative statements. They are sharing their intuitions with others and, given a supportive environment and a willingness to listen attentively to others, they can rely on the Holy Spirit to guide them.

This process requires a skilled and knowledgeable facilitator, who can express the teaching of the Church in the language of the ordinary believer and create an environment where every contribution is valued. The facilitator is not there to teach but to draw out from others and help to give shape to their intuitions: to invite them to tap into their supernatural appreciation of the faith. Often the reformulations provided by a facilitator provide participants with a new way of talking about God, of doing theology.

Imperfect but Valuable

Ordinary theology is an expression of personal belief and reflects the individual's experience of living the life of faith in the world. It is a first-hand theology rooted in religious practice. It arises from an act of faith and reflects a personal, intimate perhaps, relationship with God. It can, of course be idiosyncratic, contradictory and even superstitious. There is a danger that it will become too anthropomorphic, embracing the immanence of God but ignoring the transcendence. Ordinary theology may be imperfect and influenced by cultural assumptions that cannot be easily reconciled with the teaching of the Church.[14] However, exploring the meaning behind what is said can often provide useful insights that deserve to be given a voice.

David Tracy argued that theology must be grounded in the faith life of believers in their practice and the beliefs that underpin this.[15] If theology makes no difference to how people live their lives and only provides a theoretical framework, then it runs the risk of becoming an intellectual game that rather than reducing the gap between what is taught and what is believed, increases it.

Both academic and ordinary theology have their place. Astley judges them to be interrelated and to differ only by degree rather than kind. My aim has been to distinguish between them and argue that both have a relevant and vital part to play in coming to a richer and fuller understanding of the faith. In particular, the place of ordinary Catholic theology needs to be reappraised and its value as an expression of the *sensus fidei* given fuller consideration. The ordinary Catholic theology does not claim authority. It is an expression of the *sensus fidei* at a personal level. It is more or less formed depending on a person's involvement in the life of faith. It requires refinement within a collective process of discernment and testing in the light of tradition. However, before any of this can happen, it has to be heard.

Endnotes

1   T. O'Loughlin, 'Why Study Theology? Theology as a resource in Christian Discipleship. *Pastoral Review*, Volume 15, issue 3 May/June (2019).

2   Cf. J. Astley, *Ordinary Theology. Looking, Listening and Learning in Theology*, (Farnham: Ashgate, 2002); and J. Astley & L. Francis (eds.), *Exploring Ordinary Theology. Everyday Christian Believing and The Church*. (Farnham: Ashgate, 2013).

3   Anselm of Canterbury (1033–1109), *Proslogium or Discourse on The Existence Of God*.

4   *LG*, 12.

5   *DV*, 10.

6   International Theological Commission, *Sensus Fidei in the life of the Church*, (Vatican website, 2014), n. 56.

7   Shakespeare, *Hamlet*, Act 1 scene 5.

8   L. Wittgenstein, *Culture and Value*. Translated by P. Winch, (Chicago: University of Chicago Press 1984), 5e.

9   Cf. I. McGilchrist, *The Master and His Emissary: The Divided Brain and the Making of the Western World*, (New haven and London Yale university Press, 2009).

10   I accept that this argument is highly speculative and requires much more development than a short article allows.

11   Pope Pius IX, *Dei Filius*, (Vatican website, 1870).

12   Cf. J.B. Metz, *A Passion for God: The Mystical-Political Dimension of Christianity*, Translated by J. M. Ashley, (New York: Paulist Press, 1998).

13   McBrien, *Catholicism*, p. 40.

14   Rahner, *Theological Investigations*.

15   Tracey, *The Analogical Imagination*.